Build Real Wealth In Real Estate

Learn game-changing strategies of new age real estate investing. Use the power of leverage (O. P. M) to create a unique portfolio of real estate to generate massive passive income.

Build
Real Wealth In
Real Estate

Learn game-changing strategies of new age real estate investing. Use the power of leverage (O. P. M) to create a unique portfolio of real estate to generate massive passive income.

Amjad Khan

SUCCESS
GYAN
PUBLISHING

Inking Inspiration

Title: *Build Real Wealth In Real Estate*
Author: *Amjad Khan*

Publisher: Success Gyan Publishing
A division of Success Gyan India Pvt. Ltd.
Old no:30 New no:24, Bhagirathi Ammal St,
T.Nagar, Chennai-600017
www.sgpublication.com

Printed in India

Dedication

To my wife, Meenu, and my sons Amaan, Ayaan, and Nehran.

Meenu, my first love and lifeline, your staunch support and motivation has taken me miles ahead of what I had set to achieve. You are my partner and soul mate who has shared my life unconditionally!

My adorable sons, I love you more than words can express. If I ever had an opportunity to be anything else, I would say NO as there is nothing better than being a father to the three of you. You have brought infinite positivity and happiness to my life. I am blessed to begin my days with your smiles and have my world filled with your laughter and mischiefs. Bless you...

Dedication

Table of Contents

Foreword

I met Amjad a few years ago through a common friend in the real estate business and from the first encounter, began an endearing relationship. He requested me to pen a foreword for his book, and I take great pleasure in doing so. As developers, we both are students who observe and analyze investor behavior. We have witnessed the investor's penchant for buying a second residential property but few venture into commercial and retail properties.

Amjad recently discussed his intention to write a book on educating the common man about concepts like leverage and passive income in property and creating a portfolio of real estate properties to retire early. I was pleasantly surprised. It is not often that you find a businessman willing to share his secrets with others in order to guide them toward building wealth. He has examined middle class investor behavior patterns for several years and applied his knowledge to propose bold moves in real estate investing.

Through this book, he has made a sincere attempt not only to identify common mistakes made in real estate investment but also to come up with practical solutions to wealth building. If an investor understands and applies the Property Evaluation Matrix intelligently, he can avoid buying poor properties. As an author, Amjad makes a fervent pitch to all investors to move out of their comfort zone and look at options in commercial properties, retail, and land.

"Leverage is an incredible tool in achieving financial freedom" explains Amjad—a tool that most investors are unaware of and unwilling to tap. The book does not sermonize but nudges the reader gently to change their attitude. A sentence in chapter 5 sums it up neatly. *When people look at property as an investment option, they tend to ask themselves, "Can I afford this property?" But the correct question to ask oneself is "How can I arrange down payment (seed money) and use the benefit of leverage/O.P.M to buy that property and keep my risks at minimum?"* The ideas of using leverage, O.P.M, and seed money will be popularized among the common investors with this attempt.

Going through the book, I have seen many such concepts being explained in simple terms using case studies and illustrations to enable the reader to understand them easily. I truly urge readers to take advantage of the ideas proposed in this book and implement them prudently in their portfolios to hasten the wealth building process. One doesn't need to be a great mathematician to play with figures, but one must be willing to move out of the comfort zone to build wealth and retire early. We all have a wish list to achieve and dreams to be fulfilled, so what better way than to start now?

I wish Amjad the best and success in this endeavor, and I am certain there will be many such endeavors that will benefit society at large.

UMASHANKAR MODI

Acknowledgements

Writing a book appears to be an individual project but reality is that if you want it to be read by thousands or millions of people, it takes an entire team to shape that dream.

I would first like to thank my wife, the love of my life, Meenu. Thank you for allowing me the space to do what I came here to do. I would also like to thank my parents, brother, sister, and my sons for their unending love and support.

Next, huge thank you to my senior manager, Mr. Raju Gandhi, for his hard work in making this book a reality. Without him, this book wouldn't be possible. I would also like to thank my office team especially Umesh, Aslam, and Mihir who helped to get all my hand written notes typed swiftly and against tight deadlines. My team of support staff who ran every small errand that was necessary.

I take this opportunity to thank Surendran Jaysekar, owner of Success Gyan Publishing, who inspired me to write this book. I also want to express my gratitude to the complete team at Success Gyan especially Claudia and Jyotsna for their support in making this dream a reality against impossible deadlines.

Thank you Akash Bansal for providing your valuable inputs and expertise in mathematical calculations. Thanks to Sharmila Mehendale for helping me edit the content and giving her time and energy in making this book a reality.

Thank you to my mentor, Mr. Umashankar Modi, for his ongoing guidance, support, and encouragement in this effort. Thank you to Mr. Vilas Mungekar for his motivation and help in writing my previous book.

I am grateful to Mac Attram for teaching me the concepts of passive income. Thank you to Robert Kiyosaki and Donald Trump for their books and innovative concepts on Passive Income and Leverage that have imparted incomparable insights on the topic. Thank you to Mr. Kevin Green *(The UK Property Lord)* for his guidance.

I am grateful to all the conceptualizers, trainers, and organizers of the *Peak Performance Seminar* including T. Harv Eker, Blair Singer, Robert Riopel, Tony Robbins, Karan Hasija, Rajiv Talreja. Special thanks to the owner of Success Resources, Veronica Tan.

Finally, big thank you to readers who have purchased this book to achieve property mastery.

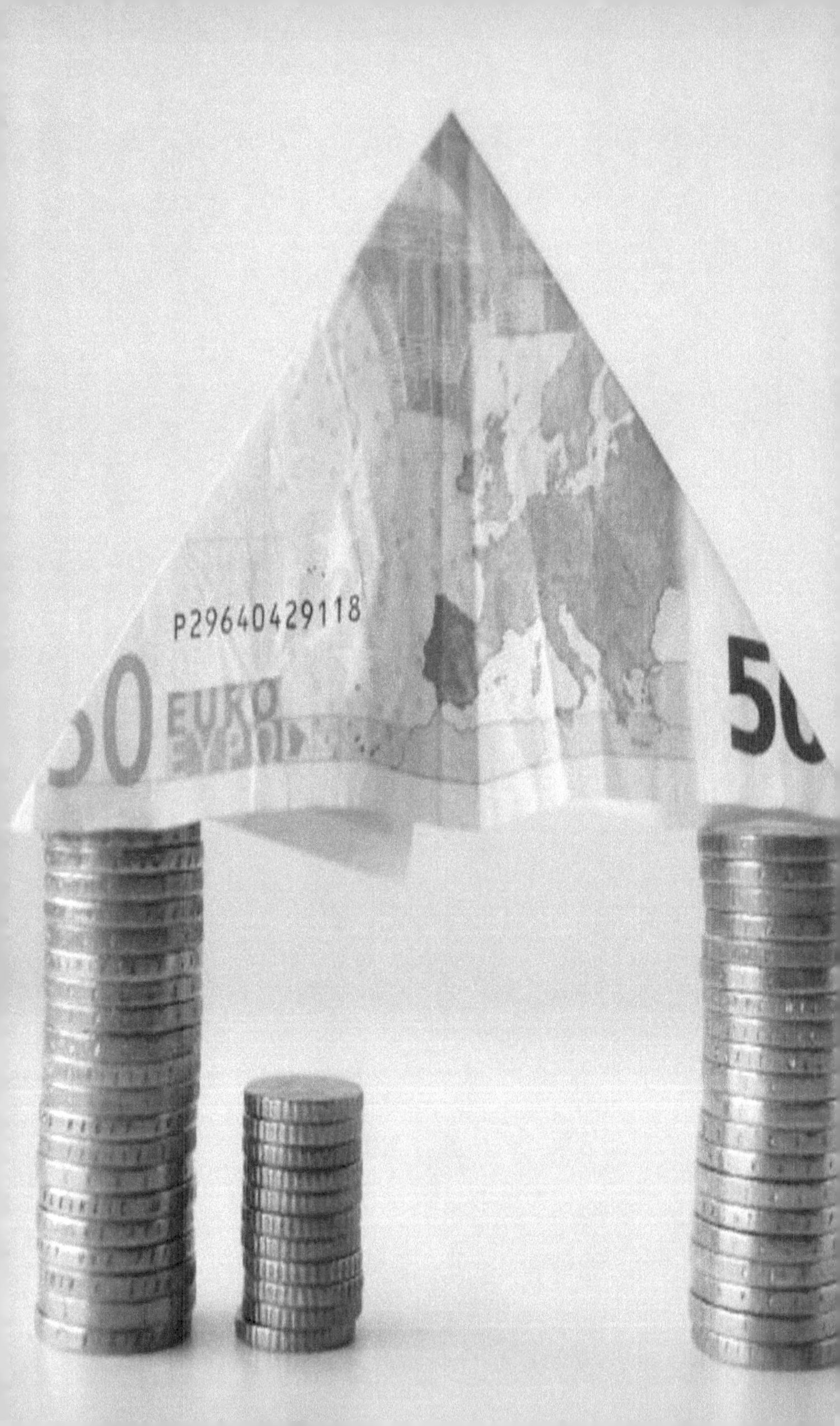
P29640429118
50
EURO
50

Chapter 1

Only Real Estate Is Real

"Buy land, they are not making it anymore"-
Mark Twain

LAND – AN INSATIABLE DEMAND, SCARCELY MET

The planet was born with a fixed area of land, abundantly filled with resources. Man discovered innumerable ways to put land to good use. Humankind is still coming up with the rising needs versus the scarcity of land as a resource. The insatiable hunger of man for this resource has however been on a perpetual upswing since the beginning of time.

Early references to humankind are replete with the exploitation of land for agricultural and residential purposes, albeit within their limited capacities. However, as the human race has exploded on the Earth, land has become invaluable to all human needs.

WHY ONLY REAL ESTATE IS REAL?

As we know, real estate is central to all human needs. Life today, revolves around the necessities that are satisfied by real estate in some form or the other. We need real estate for housing and multiple purposes like working, manufacturing, producing, commercial, retail, entertainment, hospitality, education and healthcare, infrastructural usages, recreational purposes, logistics and more.

It can safely be assumed that all of human life flourishes around real estate and it has become central to all human needs. Business can come and go, but real estate is there forever.

THE PAST LEGACIES OF REAL ESTATE, A PROVEN GOOD INVESTMENT

In the past, individuals have invested in land as a traditional asset. The same land that was purchased by our ancestors for a few thousand rupees a few decades ago, is currently worth several lakhs of rupees. One acre of land bought in 1975's for INR 5 lakhs is worth INR 40 crores today. Another example can be the individuals who have invested in a one BHK apartment in a city like Mumbai/ Pune fifteen years back. They may have purchased their flats for INR 10 lakhs, but today the same investment is worth more than a crore. These kind of phenomenal returns given by real estate, have not only beaten inflationary trends and given positive returns; such returns are unseen in any other investment.

> *"Real estate is an imperishable asset, ever increasing in value. It is the most solid security that human ingenuity has devised. It is the basis of all security and about the only indestructible security."*
> *– Russell Sage*

THE PRESENT SCENARIO OF REAL ESTATE

In the last few years, an excessive supply of residential properties as against its suppressed demand, have resulted in negative growth and returns in the housing sector. Commercial properties however, are free from these issues. The prices are more realistic and the supply is limited as compared to its demand, making it a buyer's market. The rentals earned on commercial properties are still very attractive vis-à-vis the rent earned on residential properties. This makes commercial properties a more attractive investment option, and I will discuss ways and means to select this option logically and wisely to make it a part of your portfolio.

> *"When I am asked, is real estate a good investment? My reply is, I don't know. Are you a good real estate investor?"*
> *– Robert Kiyosaki*

THE FUTURE OF REAL ESTATE

Fast paced urbanization has led to a large influx of people to the mega cities like Mumbai, Delhi, Kolkata, Bengaluru, Chennai, Gurugram, Hyderabad, Ahmadabad, putting a lot of pressure on the land available here, and the services expected by people from these cities. Every year 20 million youngsters are graduating in India and moving to the large cities for better opportunities, and this is adding to the growing demand for housing and other services in the urban areas. As the populations expands, the need for residential properties, schools, colleges, malls, offices, hospitals and logistics for all commercial and retail establishments is on the rise in metro cities.

"The best investment on Earth is earth."
– Louis Glickman

According to the sources, almost 40 percent of India or approximately 30 crore (300 million) people, are expected to migrate to the mega cities by 2030. This opens up infinite avenues for real estate and the future looks bright for the industry, which is likely to clock a growth rate of 20 percent p.a. over the next few years.

The real estate sector in India is one of the fastest growing one in the world. The growth is mainly attributed to the rapidly expanding population base, the accelerated urbanization pace and the enhanced income levels. The last few decades has completely changed the face of the real estate industry.

HARNESS THE TRUE POTENTIAL OF YOUR MONEY

We work very hard to earn money and after earning it, we are not careful about how we spend or invest it, to gain maximum return out of it. We have to ensure that the money for which we worked so hard, should work even harder to generate more returns for us. We need to invest that money where we can get maximum return on our investment (R.O.I).

---

*"You work hard to earn money and make sure
that the money works even
harder for YOU."*
- Amjad Khan

From investing to harvesting... let's see how your assets have performed over the last four decades. Normally we put our investment in following avenues

TYPE OF INVESTMENT	INVESTED IN 1979	VALVE ON 2016	PERCENTAGE	INFLATION (7.67 percent) ADJUSTED RETURN
F. D	1 Lakh	19.75 Lakhs	8.39	0.72
GOLD	1 Lakh	36.53 Lakhs	10.21	2.54
SENSEX	1 Lakh	2.53 Cr.	16.13	8.46
REAL ESTATE	1 Lakh	3.33 Cr.	17	9.33

Indians have traditionally invested in peculiar investment options like bank FD's, gold, stock market and real estate. Nevertheless, before we analyze how these instruments perform, let us look at the impact of inflation on investments.

INFLATION: Inflation simply put, is the general increase in prices on year on year basis (Y-O-Y) and fall in purchasing value of money. Suppose you are buying a commodity for INR 100 today and next year due to inflation same commodity costs INR 110, then you will need INR 10 more, to buy it. This means inflation is 10 percent and therefore you need to invest your money in those instruments, which can give returns of more than 10 percent p.a. to beat the inflation. Otherwise, you will get the same figure upon maturity, that you had initially invested in or may be less than that. The average annualized inflation for the above thirty-seven years period is 7.67 percent. If INR 1 lakh has been kept inside the locker at home instead of being invested, its value has come down to a mere INR 5208. We should look for *real returns*, which are returns after inflation. You can assume an inflation rate of around 5-7 percent every year in the future. Now let us look at the performance of our investments one by one.

BANK FIXED DEPOSITS: Traditionally, most Indian families park their excess cash in bank FDs because of the lowest risk factor associated with banks. How many investors have actually calculated if their FDs beat the inflation, to give a positive return? As investors, we are more focused on the safety factor and often ignore the negative returns on our investments.

FDs have given inflation adjusted return of 0.72 percent in last thirty-seven years. If we factor in the tax component, then the FD would automatically turn negative, and the gold and silver would deliver negligible returns. Only real estate and equity would have provided real rate of returns of around 9 percent but in the case of equity, we should have directly invested that amount in sensex.

GOLD: Gold is an asset that is passed on from one generation to the other. India is the largest consumer of gold in the world, as Indians believe in the safety and value addition to owning gold as an asset. Though gold has increased in value over the years, the younger generation is uninterested in this investment.

Gold has given an inflation adjusted return of 2.54 percent over the last thirty-seven years, which is much lower in comparison to return generated by real estate within the same period that is 9 percent. Though we can invest in gold for our social needs, ideally it should not be more than 5 to 10 percent of our portfolio. Besides, when we liquidate this asset to the jeweler, we end up losing 10 percent of the amount as depreciation. It is also a tangible asset, which we normally liquidate in case of an emergency.

EQUITIES: Sensex, born in 1979, gained popularity among the investors from the mid 80's but it needs a well-informed risk taker to invest money in the stock, due to the extreme fluctuating and volatile nature of the stock exchange.

"But land is land, and it's safer than the stocks and bonds of Wall Street swindlers."
– Eugene O'neill

Over the last three decades, some stocks have given very good returns in comparison to real estate, but a small percentage of a wise few people have been fortunate to get the benefits, and a majority of them lose money in stocks. This is probably because we need market study, the knowledge of numbers and the market research to select, buy and hold those shares. We also need to time the market to exit with profits; we need to hold a long-term perspective while investing in certain stocks, which can give handsome returns over time.

Since its inception in 1979, the sensex has given returns of around 16.13 percent in last thirty-seven years (1979 to 2016). Even after adjusting it to inflation, it has returned 8.46percent, which is good in comparison to Gold or FD's, which gave a 0.11 percent return in the same period. However, you have to keep in mind that above is the performance of the sensex, for which you should have directly invested in sensex instead of buying shares of any particular company.

MUTUAL FUNDS: The mutual fund industry is a relatively newer concept, which flooded the market in the early 90's. It caught the investor's fancy as it opened an indirect route to the stock market for all small investors who were risk averse. Over a period, the MF industry grew by leaps and bounds and became an attractive option to park excess funds available with the investors.

Mutual funds investments through the SIP route is a good strategy as some of the best Mutual funds have delivered up to 15-17 percent returns in the long term. However, most people don't apply the due diligence while investing in MFs, because we try too hard to time our equity investments. We struggle to retain the conviction to continue our SIPS when equity markets slump. We are also tempted to pull out or liquidate our mutual funds whenever we face an emergency or we want to make any lifestyle acquisitions.

TRADITION LIFE INSURANCE POLICY: Most people do not know the difference between insurance as protection, and insurance as investment. That's why they buy traditional life insurance policies like endowment or money back plans, which not only offers an inadequate cover at a high premium but also give poor returns (5-6 percent) that does not beat inflation. The best option is to buy a term plan, which is a pure protection instrument, (you can get a cover of 1 Cr. for as low as INR 10,000 p.a.) and for your long-term goals, you invest in real estate or mutual funds.

Before we discuss the last instrument, which is real estate, let us understand the psychology of the consumer. Investors have a peculiar behavior pattern and we must understand this behavior to realize how it impacts the investment trends.

INVESTOR'S BEHAVIOR: Investments returns is not *Investor's return*. One thing you need to understand clearly is that there is a difference between investment return verses investors return. For example, the sensex has given an inflation adjusted return of around 9 percent in thirty-seven years and certain MFs have given inflation adjusted return of 9 percent. However, for you (Investor) to achieve those returns you should have done two things. First, you should have invested your amounts directly into to Sensex (99 percent of people do not do that) or in those mutual funds which performed best. Second, you should have stayed invested for thirty-seven years in the sensex and twenty-two years in mutual funds to achieve that kind of returns but again 90 percent people do not do that. Real estate has an edge over other investments because people remain invested in real estate for very long period of time, and so they are able to reap the rewards of long term investment.

REAL ESTATE: This leaves only real estate as the most favored destination for families to invest their hard-earned money. Indian families have loved to invest in land and houses, and often these are passed on as heirlooms from one generation to the other.

"Buying real estate is not only the best way,
the quickest way, the safest way, but the only
way to become wealthy."
– Marshall Field

However, there is no reliable long-term data available for the performance of real estate in the same thirty-seven years but there are numerous examples available wherein real estate has given a return of 10 to 20 percent in last thirty-seven years. In addition, real estate is a tangible asset, which you can touch, feel and enjoy or have control over it; which is not the case with other paper investments where you have no control at all. The advantage of real estate is that you invest bigger amounts in real estate and hold it for long period; you don't generally sell it when market is not moving. Due to the tendency of holding onto it for longer period, you get very good returns in the long term. In some instances, it's been passed as heirlooms from one generation to the other. Another benefit of real estate is that it can generate an ongoing steady passive income (rental income) up to 10 percent p.a. At the same time, your capital value also appreciates, which is not the case with other investments. You can even get Income Tax benefits if you take a house loan to buy the property. The major plus point of real estate is that it's the only investment where you can borrow other people's money (O.P.M) to purchase and control income producing property. You can put just 20 percent of the amount and borrow 80 percent money from banks, to leverage the investment capital into more property rather than purchasing one, on full down payment. The power of leverage magnifies your overall rate of return and accelerates your wealth creation.

"Ninety percent of all millionaires become so through owning real estate."
– Andrew Carnegie

"It's tangible, it's solid, and it's beautiful. It's artistic from my standpoint and I just love real estate."
– Donald Trump

Since we are dependent on real estate for various purposes like living, working and investing; our investment in real estate is significantly higher than any other investment we make. Therefore, it's very important that we should learn more about how to buy and select the right real estate which will give highest return on our investment (R.O.I). By taking a well-informed decision, we can save ourselves from years of hardships by not buying the wrong property.

COMPARISON BETWEEN
EQUITY & REAL ESTATE (PROS & CONS)

Real Estate	Equity
You get **Power of Leverage** (Bank Loan) to buy Real Estate while you pay **10%** amount as **Down Payment (DP)** you get Loan upto **90%.** You own and control **100%** value of the property.	You have to make **100%** investment. You can't buy Reliance Shares at today's price promising to pay Reliance small amounts every month for the next 20 years.
Real Estate gives regular cash flow by way of **Rent** every month. You get **6 to 10% Rent pa** on Property Value in case of Commercial Properties.	In Equities, you can get cash flow by way of dividends but the amount is very negligible hardly **1 to 2%.**
Real Estate Market is mostly stable. It always goes up but sometimes it can see a correction to the tune of **10 to 20%.**	Equity market is very Volatile. Sometimes the value of equity can go down by upto **90%.** So chances of making losses is very high.
You get Tax Benefits in Real Estate.	You **don't get** any **Tax Benefit.**
People invest big amounts in Real Estate and remain invested for longer period of time due to that they get good returns on their investment in the long term.	Generally people invest less amount in Equity **(10,000 to 20,000 in SIPs)** and majority of them don't remain disciplined and invest for long term. They withdraw money for emergencies. So they get less returns.
On an average **more percent of people** make money in Real Estate.	On an average **less percent of people** make money in the Share Market.
Real Estate is based on **principles.**	Share Market investment is investment made on **speculation.**
You own and control the Real Estate. You can use the property yourself or you can give it on Rent.	Most people are unable to deal with extreme up and downs of the market and it can adversely affect their health.
There is **Less Liquidity** in Real Estate	**Liquidity is more** in Equities.

KEY TAKE AWAY :

For creating lasting wealth and health, tap the Real Estate (by using the principles taught in the book). For liquidity in portfolio, use Mutual Fund / Equities.

My mission is to educate people on how to become *Masters in Real Estate Investment* so that they can make more money than ever before, and become financially well off in life as early as possible.

"Now, one thing I tell everyone is learn about real estate. Repeat after me: real estate provides the highest returns, the greatest values and the least risk."
– Armstrong Williams

WHAT YOU WILL LEARN IN THIS BOOK

- How to earn tons of money within very short time and become financially free.
- The questions that we need to ask before we buy any real estate
- How to select the best property for investment and self use
- How to calculate the (R.O.I) return on investment before buying any property
- How to use the power of leveraging (O.P.M) in buying properties
- How to make portfolio of properties to generate massive passive income
- Parameters to apply before we buy any property
- Due diligence to do (paper work) before we buy any property
- How to maintain our investment properties

- We can learn from the live example of people who have made good money by using the principals mentioned in this book

---

*"Watch, listen and learn. You can't know it
all yourself. Anyone who thinks they do is
destined for mediocrity."*
– Donald Trump

All figures herein above (except real estate) are taken from wisewealthadvisors.com (1979 to 2016)

Chapter 2

Emerging Opportunities in Real Estate

> *"Buy real estate in areas where the path exists...and buy more real estate where there is no path, but you can create your own."*
> – David Waronker

The Indian population is growing at the rate of 1.8 percent p.a. per 1.60 crore people per annum and to sustain this population, the real estate has to cater to the booming demand for houses. The burgeoning population makes a race to the cities searching for employment opportunities but adding to the woes of the city.

Three hundred million Indians are expected to move to urban areas over the next 20 years. That means India will be 40 percent urban by 2030. It is estimated that the rapid urbanization in the country will require the construction of 700 to 900 million square meters of commercial and residential space.

70 percent of these cities are not yet built. 70 percent of almost everything water systems, the houses and infrastructure, are not yet built. Not the population; the population is there. So we have a rare chance of designing it right."- Shirish Sankhe, a director in McKinsey's Mumbai office had reported.

TYPES OF REAL ESTATES

In the backdrop of the above factors, we can categorize the Real estate industry into five main sections:

- Housing
- Retail
- Commercial
- Hospitality
- Open land

"Every person who invests in well-selected real estate in a growing section of a prosperous community adopts the surest and safest method of becoming independent, for real estate is the basis of wealth."
– Theodore Roosevelt

In this chapter, I will discuss with you how the paradigm shifts in the real estate sector have become apparent and the multiple choices that are developing on the scene. We can look for, understand and grab the opportunities outside the bouquet of residential investments alone.

HOUSING AND RESIDENTIAL REAL ESTATE

Housing is central to the existence of man's needs. In the last few decades, we have seen that in the metropolis, people initially lived in small apartments and stand-alone houses which were either owned or rented by them. The mega cities also had luxurious localities with bungalows and villas for the rich. Example, Jubilee Hills or White Fields in Bengaluru, Malabar Hills or Juhu scheme in Mumbai, Banjara Hills in Hyderabad, Lutyen's Delhi. The slums and chawls co-existed with the plush localities in every city.

THE CHANGING FACE OF MEGA CITIES: TIER 2 AND 3 CITIES

Development has caught up fast with the cities and is changing its skyline. The nouveau rich are moving toward the suburbs and so the face of the suburbs is getting metamorphosed. Investors who earlier invested in 1BHK flats are now seeking 1- 10 crore residences. Cities like Pune, Mumbai, Chennai, Bengaluru, Hyderabad and Ahmedabad are stretching at the seams and creating mega townships on the outskirts. In the tier 2 and 3 cities, individuals are opting for gated communities offered as individual N.A. plots with amenities. On the distant outskirts of mega cities like Mumbai; destinations like Badlapur, Khardi or Titwala are fast developing because of a new class of first time investors scouting for apartments and compact homes.

Stand alone houses in mega cities have now given way to high rises, residential complexes, gated communities offering plots, row houses and villas. From the humble 375 sq.ft. BHK to 5000 sq.ft. 5BHK luxury homes, duplexes in skyscrapers, the city offers it all.

THE EMERGING TREND ON THE RESIDENTIAL SCENE

Service apartments, hostels and housing for the senior citizens are the new sectors that are seeing a demand in driven growth. Both the concepts are relatively fresh on the residential housing sector but are poised to grow significantly in the future.

Senior Citizen Housing: A large number of elders are seeking out senior citizen homes with all facilities and services, so this segment is pushing the demand. Emergence of nuclear families and growing urbanization has given rise to several townships that are being developed to take care of the elderly and a large number of senior citizen housing projects are being planned.

Service Apartments: Service apartments have ready furniture and fixtures with a small kitchen, microwave, fridge and a washing machine provided with the apartment. It is preferred by corporate travelers visiting the city for business as well as the foreign tourists who are on tour of the city. Compared to hotels, the service apartments are more economical and spacious. Service apartments can be in a small 1BHK/2BHK flat in a housing society (you need to have permission from your society for the same) or if your budget permits, you can buy or construct an entire building after having a fixed number of service apartments.

Hostels: A large influx of students come to the metro cities to study while graduates from smaller towns come for jobs in the in BPO and telemarketing industries or corporate sectors in mega cities. They need a space and live on rental share basis (where four to six people share one accommodation) opening up a new avenue for business. We have to provide basic furniture with single bed or bunk beds and earn by charging rent on per person basis. If a 1 BHK apartment earns rent of INR 10,000 per month for an individual family, we can earn INR 16000 per month (INR 4000 per person) for the same 1 BHK by placing two single beds in the living room and two single beds in the bedroom. If the budget permits, we can build entire hostel building in the proximity of any good educational institute where students come from abroad to study or we can build the same near major IT Park or near any major business district.

"Real estate cannot be lost or stolen, nor can it be carried away. Purchased with common sense, paid for in full, and managed with reasonable care, it is about the safest investment in the world." – Franklin D. Roosevelt

---

WHAT DO WE UNDERSTAND FROM THIS?

Investors who had purchased residential flats a decade back, are reaping the rentals from these investments due to considerable appreciation; but thereafter some factors disturbed the residential real estate and the prices sky rocketed to such an extent that the cost of acquiring a residential property made no sense after looking at the rent to price ratio (R/P ratio) in the current market. I will discuss more about this in the coming chapter. I feel affordable housing, row houses in tier 2 and 3 cities are emerging as prudent investment choices for individuals provided they meet certain parameters that we are going to discuss in the coming chapter.

COMMERCIAL SPACES

EMERGENCE OF BUSINESS DISTRICTS IN INDIA

Commercial spaces comprise of small medium and large offices ranging from 300 sq.ft. to a few thousand sq.ft. depending upon the need of the organization. Post independence, larger metros in India developed some localities as commercial districts e.g. Nariman Point, Ballard Estate or BKC in Mumbai or CBD area on M.G. Road in Bengaluru or Connaught Place in New Delhi. Entrepreneurs preferred to buy or rent offices in the business districts as it promoted economies of location and encouraged the supplementary service providers to set shop around these districts. Organizations large and small, invested in offices, galas, shops and go-downs sold here. Trade and commerce flourished but it demarcated the cities into specific residential and commercial zones.

COMMERCIAL BUILDINGS UNFURL ON THE CITYSCAPE

In the 2000's however, the picture started changing. Developers started constructing stand-alone commercial buildings, business parks, logistic parks and commercial arenas right in the middle of cities and blurred the lines between commercial and residential areas. Offices evolved in residential buildings as well as commercial buildings.

Today, there is a growing demand for commercial spaces for bpo's call centers, IT offices, multi-specialty clinics and small hospitals, SMEs, spas, coaching classes, gyms, preschools, offices of professionals and a host of such enterprises within city limits, and the demand is briskly picking.

Well-maintained industrial parks with galas of varying sizes are coming in smaller suburbs. In addition, there are rising opportunities to invest in goods storage warehouses ranging from 1000 sq.ft.upto1 lakh sq.ft.

THE FUTURE BELONGS TO INVESTMENT IN COMMERCIAL PROPERTIES

"Harness the true potential of your money."
– Amjad Khan

There is a great scope for investors to invest in commercial spaces, than ever before due to the increasing demand and short supply of these spaces, giving it one of the best R/P ratio in comparison to the returns on residential real estate. In addition, the prospects look extremely bright in the near future as compared to residential properties.

The future belongs to the prudent investors who make a smart choice, and invest in commercial options which are rising on the frontier. Where can you invest?

- Retail Shops
- Pre leased office spaces
- Small to big office spaces in well managed office buildings as per your budget

- Warehouse space in well managed complex near major cities
- Industrial gala in well managed industrial parks
- Co-working Space

Pre leased offices: Office places that are already furnished and rented out by the owner, can be bought and rent can be collected from the next day onwards. Thus, you are saved of the effort of furnishing the place and finding a tenant for the same. Banks offer special rates under L.R.D (lease rent discounting) scheme for such pre-leased spaces

Offices: You can buy offices in well-managed office buildings as per your budget. In some localities, the developers offer a small to medium office that fits within the budget of 25 lakhs to 2-3 crores, which is required by small to medium entrepreneurs. If your budget permits, you can buy big pre-leased office spaces, which is generally a full floor and leased to big corporations. We have seen that big corporate entities like Tata, Birla, Adani and Mahindra do not own their office spaces but rent the place for three to twelve years, which is good for the owner. I have my investments in a medium to big pre leased offices, which I bought using O.P.M (Banks money) especially by availing lease rent discount (L.R.D) scheme of the bank.

Warehouse: You can also buy warehouses in well-managed logistic parks near you city depending on your budget. Generally, these are available in sizes of minimum 1000 sq.ft. to 1 lakh sq.ft. They normally give a good rental return of around 7 to 10 percent p.a.

Industrial Park: This concept is catching up very fast, wherein instead of having small or scattered individual factories, the SME's are buying or renting places, in well managed industrial parks for their production facilities. You can buy them as per your budget and rent it out to SME's.

Co-working Spaces: If you have a big office space in a good business locality, then instead of renting it to single person you should make a number of small cubicles and rent it out to several people. It is the best way to maximize your returns from that investment. Of course, you will have to keep staff for management but your earning will certainly increase! Besides, it's a good way to help small, medium entrepreneurs and the solo-preuneurs. You can study about this more, by looking at places working on the same concept of *Regus* and *We Work* where people can rent desk space, or a table space on rent for shorter than a month or up to a year as per their requirement.

Storage War: If you watch the series *Storage War* on History TV, you will know what I am talking about. It's a cluster of small storage spaces of different sizes (5x10 ft/10x10 ft) where a person can keep his belongings in secure manner. They are normally for those items that a person doesn't have space for, at home. He keeps his entire furniture and fixtures at such facility. If you apply the same concept to today's changing world, you will realize that even small shop owners can keep their inventory in it. The SME's can also use them to keep their extra files and important documents for which they don't have spare space in the office. You can buy small plot on outskirt of city and start this concept, it will reap rich dividends in the future.

RETAIL

Another interesting trend catching up in India is the growing idea of organized retail comprising of the whole gamut from single standalone shops to mega size shopping malls. Retail as we knew it forty years back was a fragmented, distributed and sharply divided into the organized and unorganized sectors. The organized sector was dominated by the mom and pop shops, the kiranawalas, the chemists, cloth stores or the other utility shops, while smaller paan or repair shops would comprise of the unorganized sector.

The retail scene started revolutionizing with changing demographics, rising incomes and the mall culture. The early twentieth century saw the government open up retail up to 100 percent FDI and this completely transformed the way retail business was conducted in India. Soon we saw the birth of malls, and small super markets and branded retail in our neighborhoods.

The ground and first floors of the colonies started becoming the new mini markets and commercial outlets for numerous retail activities.

THE NEW AGE RETAIL FORMAT

The Indian retail industry is one of the growth engines of the economy clocking 10 percent growth of the GDP and employing 8 percent of the labor. Shopping malls and big multi-brand retail outlets like Big Bazaar, Star Bazaar, D'mart, Reliance Trends, Chrome, Titan and FBB are changing the model of retail business. According to a report released by FICCI in 2011, the growing middle class and their changing aspirations are the reasons of their new age retail developing in the country. Moreover, most interestingly, the growth is now driven by the organized sector. Retail outlets in large malls, hypermarkets and super markets as well as retail spaces on the ground floor or the first floor of road touch complexes, are the emerging investment opportunities that I can identify here.

Due to the emergence of multi brand retail formats, this industry also needs a back-ups in form of supply chain management, logistics management, back end operations support and technological support that drives the back end industry.

EMERGING OPPORTUNITIES TO REAP RICH
RETURNS IN RETAIL

There are many new housing complexes coming up in affordable housing segment. To service the residents of these complexes, retail spaces are also coming up. You can also buy a shop in a shopping complex where branded retails shop are coming up. I would personally suggest that you should buy shops coming up on main roads and this is the kind of investment that would never fail. You can even start your own business in such kind of shops, by taking the franchisee of any big brand. Don't buy property in a mall because it's a risky investment.

RETAIL SPACE ON THE FIRST FLOOR

While granting sanction to buildings facing the main roads, normally sanction is given for retail shops on the ground floor and commercial space on first floor and above that are the residential apartments. You can buy a shop if you are getting it at reasonable price and if your budget permits, you can also invest in commercial spaces on the first floor, which is ideal for small hospitals, consulting rooms for doctors, gyms, yoga/aerobic classes, coaching classes, wellness centers, pathology labs, fine dining restaurants etc.

"Build real wealth in real estate."
– Amjad Khan

HOSPITALITY AND ENTERTAINMENT

"Athithi Devo Bhava" is the longstanding caption of India's hospitality and tourism industry. India is a multi-ethnic, multi cuisine country, proud of their culture. Guests are treated as God, and so the hospitality and tourism industry in India is truly exceptional in its character. Equally matchless is the entertainment industry in India. It is a home to mainstream Bollywood and several regional film industries and together they thrive as one of biggest film producing industries of the world. Hospitality, resorts and cinema theatres make up an extraordinary trio of this chapter.

DYNAMICS OF CHANGES IN HOSPITALITY AND ENTERTAINMENT

Since the 1990s, we have seen rapid developments in the service sector in India that revolutionized the tourism and entertainment industries. The debut of amusement parks, water parks and cinema complexes were seen in the entertainment arena. The dawning of adventure tourism resorts, spiritual tourism destinations, numerous wellness centers, destination wedding resorts, Ayurveda/Panchkarma centers, spas and other holistic curing businesses, flooded the tourism industry.

EMERGING OPPORTUNITIES IN HOSPITALITY

- Weekend bungalow / Resort apartment projects
- Service apartments / Air BnB's etc.
- Renting Open land for tent stay or weddings
- Revenue share model of resort/ hotels

"It is a comfortable feeling to know that you stand on your own ground. Land is about the only thing that can't fly away."
– Anthony Trollope

WEEKEND BUNGALOW PROJECT

You can invest in weekend bungalow projects, wherein you can enjoy your property at weekends and earn rental income the rest of the year.

AirBnB:

The latest trend in the market are tourists preferring to stay at somebody's home due to advent of popular online portals like AirBnB and Stayzilla, as it is more economical and gives a sense of *Homeliness* to the tourist. You can become the host by registering yourself on these portals and renting out your flats on a daily basis. It equips you to earn a higher income, as compared to renting out your flat to somebody on lease and license.

Tent Stays or Tree Houses

If you have an open plot of land near any tourist place, you can just put some tents there and earn a handsome income by putting that plot or land to good use. You can also coordinate with an adventure tourism company for regular business. This concept is being lapped up in many tourist destinations across the country. You can put a lawn in your plot and put it up for rent as an open lawn for marriages.

Revenue Share model in a resort or hotel

This concept is also catching on in India wherein the developer builds a resort comprising of a certain number of cottages, bungalow or rooms. He then sells those cottages to individual buyers and thereafter he runs the resort or hotel on the revenue sharing method, where he takes 30 to 40 percent of the revenue for maintenance and management of the resort, and distributes the remaining amount equally among the number of unit holders. This is a good shot at having your share in hospitality sector and earning regular passive income while your capital also appreciates.

OPEN LAND

To carry out future infrastructural development in a planned manner, the Indian Government is carrying out the exercise of *zoning* work; that is categorizing the defined uses of almost all lands in India.

"He is not a full man who does not own a piece of land."
– Hebrew Proverb

Zoning work of lands falling under urban areas is done by the Local Municipal Corporation. The zoning work of rural areas is done by the regional planning department and governed by the Assistant Director of Town Planning (ADTP) whose office is located in every district (Generally inside collector office) and usually those lands are categorized into the following zones:

1. Residential Zone
2. No Development Zone
3. Agriculture or Green Zone
4. Forest Zone

Precautions to take while buying a piece of land: While buying any land, you must first check the applicable zone under which such land is categorized, to ascertain the kind of development that you are permitted to carry out on that land. Ideally, it is safe to buy (**Non Agricultural Land**) N.A. land. There are different types of N.A. lands:

N. A. – Commercial N. A. – Warehouse N. A. – Resort N. A. – IT N. A. – Residential

WHAT DOES IT MEAN FOR THE BUYER?

If a plot of land is type N.A. residential that means we can build a residence there, but can't make any commercial shop or office there for other N.A. types. You can buy the N.A. – Residential plot for investment purposes or for building your home. You can buy the N.A. – Commercial plot for building the commercial building, shopping mall, office complex, retail shop, cinema theater, hospital, educational institutes. Simply put, the exploitation of land depends upon the category of land you purchase.

"Buy on the fringe and wait. Buy land near a growing city! Buy real estate when other people want to sell. Hold what you buy!"
– John Jacob Astor

It is risky to buy an open land without N.A. status due to various legal problems, which can crop up later. I suggest that you do not to get into it, unless you have previous experience of the same. Even before buying N.A. plots, go through my chapter on due diligence.

The idea of this chapter is to make you aware of numerous opportunities available in different sectors of real estate, so instead of looking at residences as real estate as a whole, you can explore multiple options available in the segment & can get benefitted by the same.

SUMMARY

Instead of investing your money in residential realty, you can invest it in following options:

- Retail Shops
- Pre Leased Office Spaces
- Offices in Commercial Buildings
- Commercial Space on the 1st Floor
- Weekend Bungalows and Apartments

- Studio Apartments
- N.A. Plots / Land in yellow zone
- A Flat in the affordable Housing Segment
- Warehouse/ Factory Shed/ Go-downs
- Industrial Gala
- Resort and Hotels on Rent Back scheme
- Hostels or Service Apartments

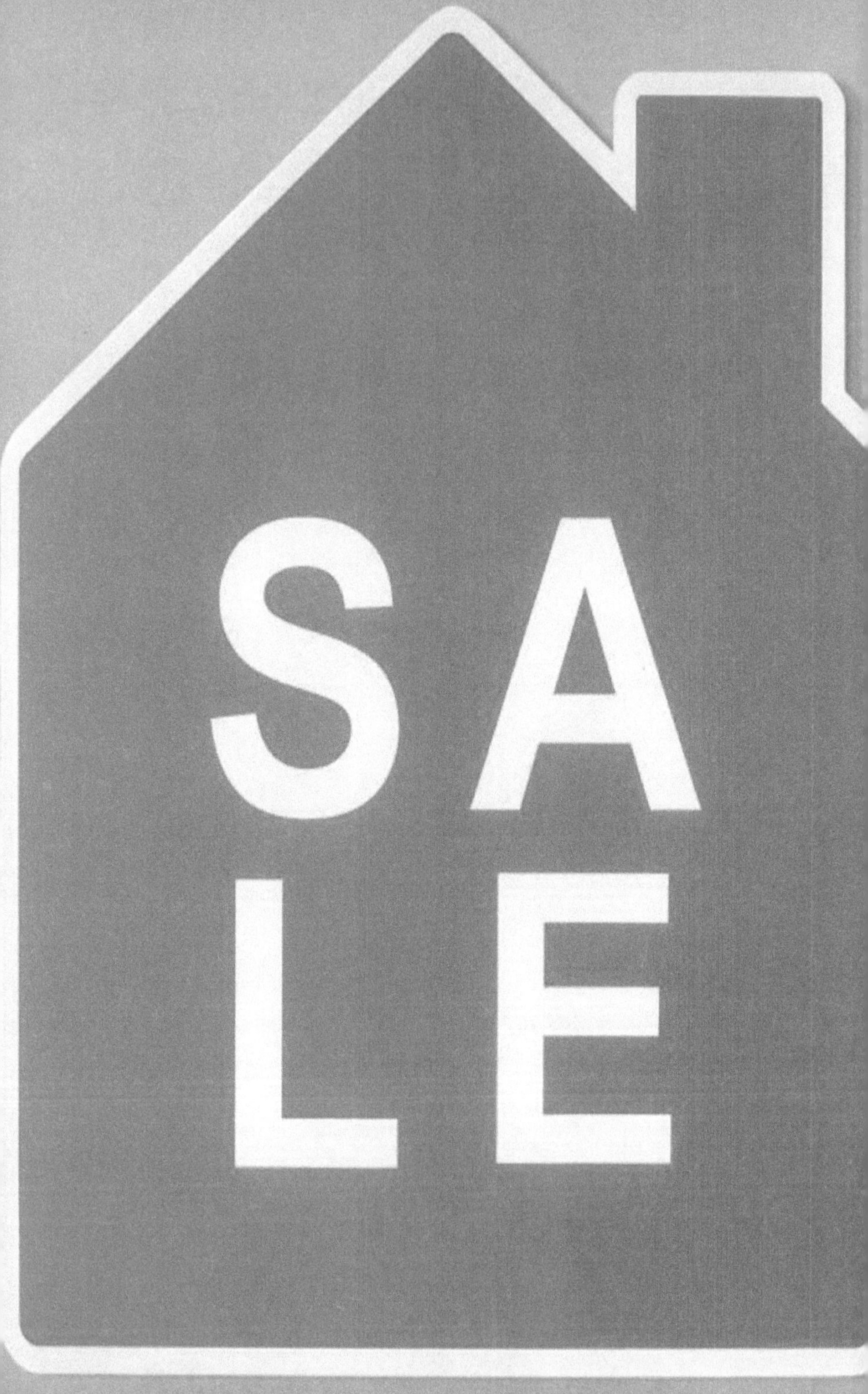
SALE

Chapter 3

How to Select the Ideal Property?

"The individual investor should act consistently as an investor and not as a speculator" Ben Graham

---

PROPERTY - A BASIC HUMAN WANT

We invest our hard-earned money in buying properties either for self-consumption (home/ office/ shop/ factory/ recreation purpose) or purely for the purpose of investment. Since a major portion of our money is utilized in buying these types of properties, it is imperative to learn how to select the real estates, which will bring the maximum returns on our investments.

As a prudent investor, one needs to *analyze the relative value* of several properties before zooming in to select the options of investment. The Real Estate market offers multiple investment opportunities for customers in terms of Under Construction Homes, Stand Alone Houses, Duplexes, Quadplexes, Rental Properties, Commercial Properties Bungalows, Villas / High Value Homes, N.A. plots etc. However, before you zoom in on a property, it's impertinent to ask ourselves the question given below.

BEFORE MAKING AN INVESTMENT IN ANY PROPERTY, WHAT ARE OUR EXPECTATIONS?

Please (✓) the appropriate Box

Negative Returns over the years	
Average Returns	
Best Returns	
Outstanding Returns	

If we expect outstanding returns on our investment, we need to understand how to select those properties that generate outstanding returns. We also need to know how to calculate which property is giving the best **R.O.I.** In properties, we earn Return on Investment (R.O.I) in the following two ways:

- By way of appreciation in the Property Value over the years
- By way of regular rental returns (Cash flow / Dividends)

To ensure outstanding appreciation and best rental returns (cash flow) on our property, we will however have to apply certain criterion while selecting it. I will give you ideas and mechanisms that will help you select the ideal property.

TEN TIPS TO MAKE A WELL INFORMED CHOICE:

- Rent / Price ratio (R/P ratio)
- Location
- Current Status of Property
- Population Growth
- Job and Economics
- Accessibility
- Safety and Crime Rates
- Limitation on Supply
- High Demand Areas
- Maintenance and Upkeep

"The property you looked at today and wanted to think about until tomorrow may be the same property someone looked at yesterday and will buy today."
– Koki Adasi

RENT / PRICE RATIO

The Rent to Price ratio or the R/P ratio is like P/E ratio in equities. It's an easy way to evaluate a property for its economic efficiency.

To calculate rent to price return ratio, we should take the total rent earned in a year, divide it by the total cost and then multiply it by 100 to arrive at exact percentage of return. For example, there is a housing price in a given area ABC costing us INR 50 Lakhs for 1 BHK apartment, and it is generating a rental yield of INR 1.20 lakhs p.a., (INR 10,000 per month x 12 months) so it's rent to price ratio is just 2.4 percent p.a. (1,20,000 ÷ 50,00,000 x 100). The *lower the rent to price ratio is, the worse the market for real estate investment becomes (Rental in particular).*

For example, Mumbai has rent to price ratio of just 1 to 3 percent in residential sector. In other words, a property worth 2 crores will deliver a rent of only INR 30,000 per month. On the other hand, commercial property has a rent to price ratio of 6-10 percent; we can receive a rent of INR 1 Lakh per month on commercial (office premises) property worth 2 crores.

To calculate the correct R/P ratio deduct all incidental expenses like property tax and maintenance charges from the rent, and then calculate the R/P ratio. Sometimes you get a lower R/P ratio in a property, but there is a more chance of appreciation in the future in that property. For e.g. if you are buying a retail shop in an upcoming locality and its current R/P ratio is less compared to another property, but if there are more chances of its appreciation in future compared to the earlier one, then the property giving the higher R.O.I should be your choice.

Although rent to price return percentage is not the only factor, this is one of the most important criteria to consider while making an investment decision. We need to balance it with the other criterion that I have suggested in this chapter.

> *"I don't believe you can ever get hurt by buying*
> *a good location at a low price."*
> *– Donald Trump*

LOCATION

As seen in all industries, the demand and supply factors are decisive in the Real Estate industry too. Location is the most crucial and important factor, while selecting any property. It commands not only the desirability and the aspirational value of an area, but also pushes up its demand for property in that area. Supplies of highly aspirational localities are always short and the homes available in such great localities will perpetually be in great demand. The condition of a property can be enhanced, its size can be altered but its location cannot be changed and this rigidity makes **location** one of the most dominant factors in property selection.

We need to ensure that the property we are selecting is centrally located, and has good schools, local markets, convenience shops etc. at a walk able distance. Always buy property in a well-established area, as most growth occurs on the perimeter of the towns and it will take time for these areas to come up. Accessibility of the property to transport centers, routes, and its proximity to the city's infrastructure helps in enhancing the short and long term value of the property. Ideally, properties that we are investing in should be in a fifteen km radius of the city center or the nerve center of large cities.

CURRENT STATUS OF PROPERTY

I very strongly urge you to buy *Ready Property only* as there are many benefits associated with it:

1) Why buy only ready property: We will be saved from years of stress because a majority of the builders don't deliver on time, due to frequent regulatory issues, delays in getting the plans sanctioned, delays in the approval for revised plans, shortage of funds/materials, dispute among partners, court orders, etc. Sometimes buildings are delayed due to inadequate bookings for the project. Currently, we see ultra large projects being planned, which comprises of many buildings and hundreds of amenities. To book and construct those buildings and complete all amenities, it takes a long span of time as anywhere between five to ten years. In short, there are hundreds of reasons as to why projects are delayed and the construction of our dream home, remains a pipe dream! Therefore, it makes perfect sense to always buy ready homes in a complex that is complete with all the proposed building amenities.

2) See it to believe it: If we select the ready property, we get the actual feel of the space and can accordingly decide whether it is sufficient for our family's requirements. A majority of the people do not get an idea of the space in terms of square feet (or meter) as written in the layout plan. While buying an under construction building, we often see only layout of the apartment and at the time of possession we end up getting rooms which appear to be much smaller than in the layout. The veritable shock of booking a roomier flat and accepting a congested one is the nightmare of hundreds of flat owners who cannot visualize the flat sizes based on plans and then struggle to accommodate the entire family into a smaller space, that doesn't deem fit for the family. Though some builders show sample flats, they are usually so well furnished that we think we will be getting a similar one but when we take possession we get entirely different flat as compared to our perception. They sometimes manipulate the carpet area or they put small size furniture to make it look spacious. Therefore, it's always important to see the same constructed flat which you are buying and not "a similar one."

3) Save on interest payment: Generally, all investors buy property availing bank loan but many make a hasty decision in freezing a purchase. We must always bear in mind that banks charge an interest on the Principal amount, until the property remains under construction. A delay in the date of possession keeps adding interest payments to the bank. We can save on interest payment, when we purchase a property that is ready. Additionally, we can generate immediate cash flow (rental income) from ready property wherein case of under construction property you pay interest until it is ready.

4) Save on GST: The investor in a property has to generally pay the following taxes: Stamp duty as applicable is payable. GST is applicable if the property purchased from the builder, is under construction. *If a **ready to move in** property is purchased from the developer who has already procured the Occupation Certificate (OC) then the Goods and Service Tax (GST) is not applicable.* Value Added Tax (VAT) also needs to be paid if it is applicable in the concerned state.

5) Better Safe than Sorry: Most investors have invested all their life's savings and pinned their hopes on the roof that they have purchased after much deliberation with the Developers. Until now, some builders have given their clients a harrowing time by delaying possession of promised flats within the stipulated time. The consumers who are individual owners are often un-united and the builders have gotten away with it easily. The justice process in our country is highly protracted and delayed, making it paramount to the justice being denied.

The recent changes in laws have brought succor to several aggrieved customers facing the prospects of delayed possession. The winds of change in the Real Estate industry have come in the of **RERA** (Real Estate Regulation Act). The aggrieved customer can approach the authority and claim interest on the payment made to the builder. In case builder has delays possession. However, there is **RERA** in many states but it will take time, money and energy to get justice. You will have to follow up with the advocate and attend on hearing dates etc. so to save all this, always buy ready property.

POPULATION GROWTH

For getting good returns on investment in property, we should always look for property in the city/ town/ suburb where the population is growing steadily. Higher demand and limited supply will lead to scaled up rents and appreciate the value of the property, when the city witnesses a long-term sustainable growth. Investments should be made in cities that have a robust industry presence, or where the government is implementing Smart City programs or large scale Infra Projects like National Highways or IT parks/ SEZs. Cities that grow moderately but positively make attractive investment destinations to park our funds. There is a scope for seizing a good property at a moderate price.

JOBS AND ECONOMICS

Values of Real Estate increase only when people who live in them have good jobs and therefore better earnings prospects. Sometimes we invest in a city, which is a commercial precinct / factory dominant, for e.g. the MIDC, and if those factories move or close down, our investment will suffer because rent will go down, and we will not be able to sell our properties at a higher value.

"Find out where the people are going and buy the land before they get there."
– William Penn Adair

Before investing or zooming in on a location, it is pertinent to study the job market and the economics of the location and consider the number of jobs in the overall market. Analyze whether the jobs and different businesses in that city are increasing or decreasing, and also whether the salaries of the employed are increasing. What type of jobs are the people having and are they adequately high paid executives, BPO employees, IT park employees in the city or low paid labors, vendors, etc.? Does the city have diversified jobs, or does it depend on only one or two industries? Ideally, we should find a well diversified sources of job creation and business generation ability in that region, it should have mix of all service sectors, manufacturing, trading, govt. jobs, import/ export, etc. before we decide to make an investment in that area. Mumbai region is the best example of this study.

ACCESSIBILITY

Accessibility is also very important factor before sealing the deal. We need to ascertain that our property is located near any railway/ metro station/ airport, or close to any local market/mall or a business district. By doing so, we ensure that its value rises skywards and we reap handsome returns, by being invested in a property that most people want to live in and would not hesitate to buy/ rent/ lease.

Neighborhoods that have an easy access to a good school, hospital, landscaped park with jogging tracks, good malls and markets, closer to highways leading in and out of cities, enjoy precedence over the other localities that do not include of such facilities. Families who are investing in properties are always search for neighborhoods offering good accessibility and ample leisure options. In vertical cities like Mumbai, Delhi, Chennai, Bengaluru, etc., accessibility plays a pivotal role in property selection.

SAFETY AND CRIME RATE

Everyone wants to live in a safe place, with a minimum propensity for crimes. Our tenants and buyers will seek the same, so always buy the property where we feel safe for ourselves, and our family.

Before we make a final decision on property, I would like to stress upon the need to check out the safety of the locality in which we are investing. Are there any peculiar crimes occurring in that area for e.g. – eve teasing / crime against small children / burglaries or petty thefts? Is it safe for young children or senior citizens to live alone and unattended in these areas? Are there any business activities in the neighborhood that may attract anti-social elements? Is travelling at night, a threat to the safety of women, due to unscrupulous goons?

It is easy to procure data on the safety aspects of any locality. We can speak to the local residents as people living in that area, and have personal and upfront knowledge about crimes in the area. We can do a little online research on crime rates and statistics of that locality, and visit it at different times of the day to notice if any nuisance exists in that locality during the day and night. This shields us from unnecessary rude shocks after buying the property. In smaller towns and tier 2and 3 cities, I strongly recommend that we should buy properties in gated communities, as most of the safety issues are addressed here.

LIMITATION ON SUPPLY

Land as we know is always limited in supply and this characteristic feature of land increases the demand for it. Land being a natural resource, its supply is non-elastic and predetermined. There is very little scope for artificial enhancement or production of land and therefore hill stations, beach destinations, and other such natural or manmade perimeters push up the land prices due to a limitation in supply.

"Don't wait to buy real estate,
buy real estate and wait."
– T. Harv Eker

Cities and towns facing a natural or manmade barrier in territorial expansion may be endowed with natural beauty for e.g. beach side villas and beach front homes will always be restricted in supply, so will a mountain view, ocean view and lake view apartments and homes. Moreover, this will ensure a perpetual price surge for these properties. Here are some of the factors, which lead to a limited supply of land:

- *Natural Borders* like sea faces, rivers, creeks, lakes, mountains and hills prevent expansion – Some cities face a natural limitation to expand their boundaries as they are closer to a water bodies and this limits their expansion to a certain point.

- *Manmade Borders* like forest area, defense area, parks or zoos and sanctuaries, which prevent expansion. Some cities have demarcations like the forest area or defense areas which prohibit residential or commercial buildings after a certain limit. Supply of land gets limited where city has a zoo or a wild life sanctuary along its borders.

- *Restriction on Development*– Zoning of towns leaves a very limited amount of areas available for residential and commercial development. Creation of zones limits supply and pushes up prices owing to constantly rising demand. The *Yellow Zone* or the *Commercial Zone* or the *Eco Sensitive Zone, which* is non-exploitable, consequently the prices are sure to surge due to supply and demand mismatch.

HIGH DEMAND AREA

We should always buy property in an area where demand is more and supply is always less. Even if you can buy small property it will be worth the investment. A small shop in a market or an office in centrally located commercial building will provide you lasting returns. While investing in residential areas, we must select areas that are in very high demand and where community is developed.

You should always buy the kind of property that you would be able to sell just within two days.

MAINTENANCE AND UPKEEP

The most important criteria while selecting property is its maintenance and upkeep in future. The value of property appreciates over the years if it is maintained in an excellent condition; and vice versa. Therefore, when we are buying apartments /offices / weekend homes, we should always ensure that it is going to be a well-maintained property in the future. As diligent buyers, we must ensure that the builder has made a provision of a corpus fund for the maintenance of the common amenities or the society has the capability and the mindset for handling the maintenance. We should also enquire with the society about their rules and regulation for renting the place because many societies do not allow bachelors, college students, actors and models as tenants. Such rules can ruin our plans of earning rental income from that property or even putting up our properties on sites like AirBnB or Nestaway.

I urge all readers to keenly go through all the criteria mentioned in this chapter before buying any property, whether it is for self-use or for investment purpose because in both the cases we are putting our hard-earned money in it and so it must generate outstanding returns for us!

"90 percent of all millionaires become so
through owning real estate"
– Andrew Carnegie

PROPERTY EVALUATION MATRIX

I have designed a property evaluation matrix which I am referring to here as **AKPEM** (Amjad Khan Property Evaluation Matrix); wherein by applying the given parameters while buying any property, you can predict whether it's a good investment or the bad one. You can accordingly decide whether to buy it or not. You can save lots of money, time and energy if you apply this evaluation matrix to any property you are intending to purchase and you can make serious wealth in long term if you buy the right property.

Following is my property evaluation matrix, based on eight parameters, where in you have to give a score on a 1 to 10 scale to each parameter and in the end, calculate the total score I have given a 30 percent weightage to R/P ratio means if you are getting a R/P ratio of 5 percent then your score will be 15 and if you are getting 10 percent R/P ratio then your score will be 30. Similarly, give appropriate scores to other parameters on the scale of 1 to 10 and calculate the total score to predict whether the property you are selecting is a poor, an average or a good investment.

POINTS	PREDICTION
0 to 25	It's a Bad Investment (don't buy it)
26 to 50	It's an Average Property
51 to 75	It's a Good Property
75 and above	It's an Excellent Property

PROPERTY EVALUATION MATRIX

Parameters		Scale	Score
RP RATIO	RP	1% 2% 3% 4% 5% 6% 7% 8% 9% 10%	
	Score	3 6 9 12 15 18 21 24 27 30	
HIGH DEMAND LOCATION		1 2 3 4 5 6 7 8 9 10	
STATUS OF THE PROPERTY		1 2 3 4 5 6 7 8 9 10	
ACCESSIBILITY		1 2 3 4 5 6 7 8 9 10	
JOB AND ECONOMICS		1 2 3 4 5 6 7 8 9 10	
SAFETY AND CRIME RATE		1 2 3 4 5 6 7 8 9 10	
LIMITATION ON SUPPLY		1 2 3 4 5 6 7 8 9 10	
MAINTENANCE/ UPKEEPMENT		1 2 3 4 5 6 7 8 9 10	
		Total Score	

SUMMARY

- Buy property that will give outstanding returns.
- Buy only ready property.
- Select a property, that will give a (R/P ratio) Rent to Price ratio of 6 percent and above.
- Choose the best location, where you will get the highest appreciation in future.
- Apply the property evolution matrix given by me before finalizing any property.

Chapter 4

What is Passive Income?

---

*"If you don't find a way to make money while
you sleep, you will work till you die"*
– Warren Buffet

INCOME GENERATION CHANNELS

Income generation is the fundamental need of all individuals, because it is the backbone of our survival. Income, fuels all commercial activities and so the struggle to create, save and invest our income is primal to all humans. All individuals are engaged in income creation using either of these two techniques.

Most of us yield incomes by doing a job or by running our own businesses and this produces *active income*. Some people invest in properties, shares, FDs or have other alternative sources of procuring income, which is *passive income.*

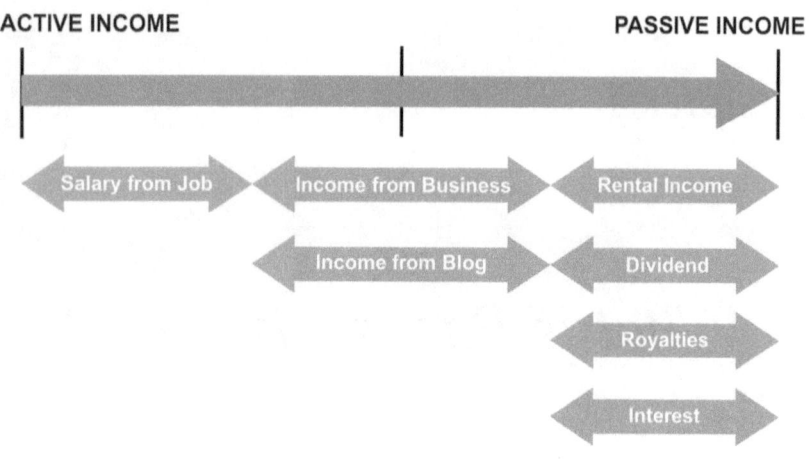

"Residual income is passive income that comes in every month whether you show up or not. It's when you no longer get paid on your personal efforts alone, but you get paid on the efforts of hundreds or even thousands of others and on the efforts of your money! It's one of the keys to financial freedom and time freedom."

AN INNOVATIVE APPROACH TO GENERATING PASSIVE INCOME

"You become financially free when your passive income exceeds your expenses."
– T. HarvEker

To make a living we work, when we are short on cash we work overtime or we do some part time jobs when we need additional funds. Have we ever wondered how and when can we get out of this rat race? We go to work and earn then spend that amount then again we go back to work! Our lives are spent coping up with this never-ending vicious circle of earning and spending. There is nothing wrong with this, but there are better avenues we can develop to make our money work harder.

We can receive income on a regular basis, with little effort on our part. When passive income is being generated, it means we are being paid every month or per annum, devoid of any active participation in the management or contributing any type of work for the enterprise and investment.

Instead of turning our time into money, there are ways to make our money grow. We can plant financial seeds that will produce income even while we are sleeping, and that is called *Passive Income.*

According to Robert Kiyosaki, the author of the book *Rich Dad, Poor Dad & Cash Flow Quadrant,* there are four different types of income worlds. According to his cash flow quadrant given below, we can study different methods by which a cash income is generated.

Let us understand each of these ideas one by one.

E: EMPLOYED, SECURE

Employees are the people who work in factories and offices to earn money. Generally, they are paid on an hourly basis, so they give their time and energy to earn money. Majority of us live our life entirely within E Quadrant. People leaving in E quadrant are perceived as just above being broke.

"Jobs are a centuries-old concept created during the Industrial Revolution. Despite the reality that we're now deep in the Information Age, many people are studying for, or working at, or clinging to the Industrial Age idea of a safe, secure job."
– Robert Kiyosaki

S: SELF EMPLOYED, INDEPENDENT

Professionals like doctors, chartered accountants, lawyers, consultants, small and medium business owners come under this category. Self-employed are the people who earn money by working for themselves or as entrepreneurs. Everybody picks on them right from their family to their employees and customers. They do not have free time and if they take the time off, they lose money. Just observe how hard doctors, advocates, CA's are working.

B: BUSINESS OWNERS, WEALTH BUILDERS

A business owner typically owns a medium to large organization, which generates money .The difference between a business owner and a self-employed person's business, is that a self-employed person works for his business but big businesses work for their owners! Typically, a big business is run by CEOs while the owner is free to take vacations or concentrate on building another big business paving way for his own empire.

I: INVESTORS, FINANCIAL FREEDOM

If you played monopoly as a child, you know how it works. Four green houses, one red hotel that taught us in early childhood to be an investor and save money if we wanted to emerge as a winner. It was a lesson that "Investors are those persons who invest their money in different income generating asset classes and create a steady flow of passive income" their money generates more money.

To conclude this analogy, I would like to impress upon all of you that our aim should be to become investor because an investor earns passive income from his investments and he has the freedom to chase all his hobbies and wishes in his free time. Read this example carefully:

"To become financially free, increase
your Passive Income."
– Amjad Khan

If you need INR 1 lakh per month for your current lifestyle and you earn that by working daily from 9 a.m. to 6 p.m. by saving some of that money on regular basis and investing it in avenues where you can generate some regular cash flow by way of interest dividend or rental income; if you are able to generate cash flow or a passive income of INR 1 lakh from your investments. You can think about taking early retirement and pursue your dreams with the unlimited free time on your hands or you can just relax and live it up.

FIVE CONCEPTS FOR TRIGGERING PASSIVE INCOME

- Interest Income On Fixed Deposit
- Dividend Income From Equities
- Lending Money On Interest
- Rental Returns From Real Estate
- Invest In Business and Become Silent Partner

"My rich dad taught me to focus on passive income and spend my time acquiring the assets that provide passive or long term residual income...passive income from capital gains, dividends, residual income from business, rental income from real estate, and royalties."
– Robert Kiyosaki

At the onset, we must realize that we need to have a large sum money to invest in the above avenues, only then will we be able to generate a steady passive income from them.

Let us suppose that there is a person **A**, who needs INR 50,000 for his monthly expenses, and if he is able to generate that amount today through passive income, then this person A is likely to retire immediately. To do so, he will need a corpus of 1 crore. (INR 50,000 x 12 months = INR 6,00,000). He will have to make an investment of INR one crore in a property that will give him R/P ratio of 6 percent returns post deductions. Therefore, that he will have rental income of INR 50,000 p.m. from property. Rental agreements have a 5-7 percent escalation clause, which helps to beat inflationary trends too.

Similarly, if same person decides to retire after ten years, he will need a monthly income of INR 98,000 (calculated with an inflation of 7 percent p.a.) to maintain the same life style that he is currently enjoying. Consequently, the corpus he would now need would be INR 1.96 Cr.

You may think it will take many years for you to accumulate the corpus amount to generate desired passive income out of it, but that is not the case.

Suppose you need a certain amount as passive income per month and you are able to get that amount by investing a large sum in an investment, which is generating R/P ratio of 6 percent p.a., how much should that sum of money be in your case? Just take a few moments to fill in the blank to work out your number or the corpus amount.

Formula to calculate the same is as follows:

Your required monthly income x 12 x 100 ÷ 6 = Lump sum corpus amount required.

Passive Income you need	Formula	Lump sum amount required
	x 12 x 100 ÷ 6 =	

For example, if you decide that today you need a monthly passive income of INR 1 lakh then at 6 percent p.a., you will need a corpus of INR 2 crores. If you want to retire in a specific number of years then you will need following amount:

Year for retirement	Corpus Required
5 Years	2.80 Cr.
10 Years	3.90 Cr.
15 Years	5.50 Cr.

Now you have become aware of the exact amount and corpus needed, the logical next step would be to create that corpus amount by investing your monthly current savings in an instrument, which will take you to your desired number in the least number of years. As you have seen, gold and bank FDs give a meager rate of return, so it will take more number of years for you to reach the desired number. The next best option is real estate where you get the power of leverage to multiply your return on investment.

Any in case of real estate, you can make down payment of 20 percent and take a bank loan for the remaining 80 percent. So by making a down payment of 20 percent, you can become the owner of 100 percent value of real estate .You also enjoy appreciation as well as rental return on the entire 100 percent of the amount. Once the loan is paid, you start getting passive rental income in your hand throughout your life. It is a proverbial case of having the cake and eating it too!

LET'S EXAMINE THE AVENUES OF PASSIVE INCOME

Bank FDs/ Bonds

Bank FD's are the most favored passive income earning strategy of most Indians, especially senior citizens. It gives a 7- 8 percent taxable return. Post tax, this return is a mere 5-6 percent, which is a negative return after inflation adjustment. They do give steady returns in form of interest for the number of years we have made the FD but our capital remains the same. If we make an FD of INR 10 lakhs with SBI for a period of five years, we will get post tax interest return of INR 5000 per month. On maturity, we will get the same amount of INR 10 lakhs back; but its value will be INR 6.95 lakhs if we consider inflation rate of 7 percent p.a., besides the rate of interest of FDs is constantly declining, as India is slowly becoming a developed country.

"How many millionaires do you know who have become wealthy by investing in savings accounts? I rest my case"
- Robert G. Allen

In near future, it could be as low as 1-2 percent p.a. as is the case with the developed nations, where they give just 0.5 percent to 2 percent interest p.a. on FDs. Data shows that due to its liquid nature, a majority of people withdraw their FD's for unplanned expenses and emergencies like children's higher education fees, vacations, medical expenses, marriage, or even for buying a nice car. Therefore, my advice to you will be to use the FD's for contingency or emergency funds, but not as a part of your strategic corpus for passive income generation.

Purchase High Dividend Stocks

By building a portfolio of high dividend stocks, we can create regular passive income and there is potential for capital appreciation. In India dividend distribution percentage is very less generally in the range of 4 to 5 percent p.a., we need to acknowledge that stocks carry market risk tag too. My suggestion will be to invest in R.E.I.T's stocks. REITS are Real Estate Investment Trusts who owns income producing real estate like commercial spaces, offices and apartment buildings, warehouses, shopping centers, hotels, etc. REITs are traded on all major exchanges, and provide investors a liquid stake in real estate. REITs have a special tax status that makes it mandatory for them to pay out almost 90 percent of their income as dividends.

We can invest in publicly traded REIT'S, which are listed on a major stock exchange by purchasing shares, or we can purchase shares of a non-traded REIT. We can also purchase shares in a REIT mutual fund. They typically provide high dividends plus the potential for long-term capital appreciation. REIT makes a good portfolio diversification. The S&P 500 Index's average annual return over the past ten years is approximately 9.14 percent, making this idea a sterling choice in our portfolio.

REIT funds will soon become reality in India; but as of now, there are no REITs funds listed in India which are available for investment for common man. We can start investing in Real Estate using this option, setting aside even small amounts as soon as REIT's become operational in India.

Lending Money on Interest
We can lend money to someone and earn a higher interest income compared to that from Bank FDs. It's risky and may not be everyone's cup of tea. You may need to procure licenses to do the same.

P2P or Peer to Peer lending is another interesting lending concept that is growing in India with many online lending platforms promoting this new generation idea. We can invest as little as INR 30,000 to get started. We can spread our investment out over hundreds of different loans if we want and can earn up to 10-15 percent p.a. as passive income.

P2P websites like faircent.com is in the practice of lending money to individuals or business through online services that match lender profiles with that of the borrowers. Just a word of caution - Please follow due diligence before investing in any of the online platforms.

Invest in Business and be a Silent Partner
Another way to earn passive income is to invest in a business and be a silent partner. This is risky, but there is potential for high return, and to reduce the apparent risks, you can invest small amounts in many companies through equity crowd funding.

In early days, only HNIs, Venture Capitalists or hardcore Angel investors would be interested to invest in startups but this concept has gradually undergone a sea change. Today, with the idea of *Equity Crowd Funding* companies have democratized the process by throwing open their doors to a larger pool of potential investors termed as *the crowd*.

A common man, who had never thought of being a small investor in a start up and enjoy the shares of a potential business success story, can now invest smaller amounts of INR 25,000 to INR 50,000 and open up another avenue of passive income for himself. In addition, the advantages of signing up as a silent partner are worth pondering about:

- You do not need to be an expert in the industry in which you are investing or participate in the day-to-day business activities of the company.
- You can invest lesser funds and bear lower or no risk in the business as compared to the active partners.
- By being a prudent silent investor, you can ensure a constant residual income stream for yourself, in short be assured of a steady passive income.

INVEST IN REAL ESTATE

"The key to financial freedom and great wealth is a person's ability or skill to convert earned income into passive income and/or portfolio income."
– Robert Kiyosaki

The biggest benefit of real estate is the surety of rental income and that is the best source of passive income. You get returns of 5-10 percent p.a. through rental income (mostly on commercial properties) plus the advantage of beating inflation due to incremental rise in rentals of 5-10 percent y-o-y. Besides that, we also get tax benefits and our property appreciates magnificently over the years, bringing forth solid long-term returns. So real estate rentals provide returns through three ways: Building equity (Value Appreciation), Delivering a cash flow (Rental Returns) and Tax Benefits.

"Use O.P.M to speed up your success."
– Amjad Khan

The power of leverage (O.P.M) plays a big role in rental property investments. If you obtain a loan to buy the property, each month your tenants are paying off a part of your loan. Once the loan on the property has been paid off, your cash flow will increase dramatically, allowing your small investment which you made in the form of down payment and the difference amount you paid (EMI Paid – Rent received) to sky rocket into a full-fledged retirement program. It would not take many such (paid off) properties to build a splendid, passive income for your family's future.

In the following chapters we are going to teach you how to effectively use the power of leverage, and how to arrange money for down payment so that you can build a *portfolio of income producing Real Estate* to help you generate passive income to retire early.

Creating a massive passive income is the holy grail of personal finance; it takes much more initial effort to start this magnum opus, such as saving judiciously and adequately to buy your first rental property. However, once you start it's easier to gather momentum. It is said that *the early bird catches the worm*, meaning the younger we start, the better we earn.

By achieving plans for regular passive income, you can do the following:

- Retire early so that you will live longer due to less stress, as per a recent survey people who retire at early age live longer life.
- Travel the world; enjoy the beauty of nature.
- Serve, contribute, do charity for a cause you truly care about.
- Spend more time with your family, children and parents.
- Find a job that may pay less, but is more interesting.
- Enjoy your time at your native place or buy your own weekend home and do some organic farming. In short, enjoy and celebrate life.
- Do the things you always wanted to do when you get free time; Follow your passion.
- Be relaxed at home; watch Netflix read good books go out to have sumptuous dinner with the family.
- Conduct seminars, share your knowledge and experience with the world.
- Write a book

Chapter 5

Leverage – Aladdin's Genie

USING THE POWER OF LEVERAGE
TO GAIN MASSIVE ROI

*"Most People never get wealthy simply
because they are not trained to recognize the
opportunities right in front of them."*
– Robert Kiyosaki.

I t is absolutely necessary to use leverage if you want to become wealthy. So what is leverage? Leverage is the act of borrowing money or O.P.M to increase potential returns. It's a truism that you need money to make money. However, it doesn't necessarily have to be your money. You can use **Other People's Money** (O.P.M) to speed up your wealth creation program. There are many types of leverage, and I will discuss them briefly with you at the end of this chapter.

- OPM - Other People's Money
- OPT - Other People's Time
- OPW - Other People's Work
- OPC - Other People's Connections
- OPE - Other People's Experiences

"Rich people choose to get paid based on results. Poor people choose to get paid based on time."
– T. Harv Eker

Though people as well as businesses across the world use different tools of leverage as mentioned above, in this book, I am focusing on the *use of leverage in Real Estate.*

HOW DOES LEVERAGE INCREASE RETURNS IN REAL ESTATE?

Leverage helps to increase the returns in Real Estate giving it the biggest advantage as an instrument of investment. In comparison to all other investment instruments, Real Estate can safely and cheaply be leveraged to increase your returns massively. It is here that you can use Other People's Money (financial institutes/ banks/ private lenders) to buy income-producing properties and can pay off the part of the debt by utilizing the monthly cash flow (rentals) that the property generates for you.

To understand how leverage works let's look at the example of two people who have INR 20 lakhs each to invest in Real Estate.

Case Study 1

Person A is an investor who has outright purchased a property for INR 20 lakhs. After paying his taxes, insurance, maintenance, property management fees, etc. his property generates a rent (cash flow) of INR 10,000 per month for him at R/P ratio of 6 percent p.a.

At the end of the year 'A' will have made INR 1,20,000 calculating 6 percent return on investment. Let us assume the property appreciated at 7 percent per year so after ten years the value of the property will be INR 40 lakhs approximately. If we add rental income, the total amount will be INR 56.50 lakhs, calculated along with a 7 percent escalation in rent on a Y-O-Y basis.

Case Study 2

Person B is an investor who bought a property worth INR 80 lakhs by investing INR 20 lakhs for down payment and taking a bank loan of INR 60 lakhs. He also got a 6 percent R/P ratio that is INR 40,000 as rental income per month, but his monthly EMI worked out to INR 77,000 p.m. So he paid INR 37,000 from his pocket to make up the difference amount.

Let us assume his property also appreciated at 7 percent per annum, so after ten years the value of his property becomes INR 1.60 Cr approximately. After deducting the amount paid toward EMI and down payment, person 'B' will receive a net gain of INR 1.13 cr. in hand. His loan is also paid up after ten years and now he is the owner of the property worth INR 1.60 crores. Additionally, he is also enjoying a monthly (passive income) rent of INR 75,000 due to increase in rent 7 percent per annum on a Y-O-Y basis.

By using the power of leverage person B is in much better financial position compared to person A and can even think about taking early retirement if he creates a portfolio of 2-3 such properties.

"Optimize Leverage, Maximize Profits."
– Amjad Khan

MORE CASE STUDIES TO HELP
YOU GAIN CLARITY ON LEVERAGE

Case Study 3

My Initial Investment: I bought a commercial property worth INR 1.5 cr. For which I put a down payment of INR 50 lakhs and I took a bank loan of INR 1 cr. for the tenure of ten years. My EMI worked out to INR 1.50 lakhs per month. I rented out this property for a rental consideration of INR 1.30 lakhs per month. I also benefitted with the escalation clause of 10 percent increase in rent per year.

How the difference works out: For the first two years, I was paying the difference amount of INR 20,000 to INR 30,000 per month toward the EMI (EMI – Rent= Difference to be paid). My EMI was INR 1, 50,000 – RENT INR 1,30,000= Difference amount INR 20,000. There after due to escalation in rent over the years, I was not paying any difference amount; instead I was getting some amount in hand after paying EMI.

The tremendous appreciation in value: Over last six years, the property appreciated in value by 100 percent; the current value of the property is INR 3 crores, while my outstanding loan amount is approximately INR 50 lakhs. If at this point I sell the property and repay the loan amount I will still get INR 2.50 cr. in hand, which is five times the return on the investment of INR 50 Lakhs. This means, within a period of just six years, I multiplied my amount by five times.

Amount in crores

Total value of property (office)	1.50
Amount paid as down payment including stamp duty, etc.	0.50
The amount of bank loan availed	1.00
The total amount paid toward EMI over six years	1.08
The amount of rent received over the year's (six years)	1.16
Sell value of the property after six years	**3.00**
Less Bank loan	0.50
Net amount in hand	**2.50**

The Advantage of Leverage: This became possible due to the power of leverage. I have a portfolio of other such properties, and have received outstanding returns on my investments. Mutual funds, bank FDs or even gold cannot give that kind of returns proving that nothing can beat the R.O.I from Real Estate!

"Leverage is an incredible tool in achieving financial freedom."
– Amjad Khan

It's the only way to build big wealth and there are not many other investments where you can do that (use the power of leverage – O.P.M). You cannot buy stocks of HDFC worth INR 1 cr. by agreeing to pay HDFC a few thousand rupees a month for next twenty years at today's price!

WHY LEVERAGE IS EFFECTIVE?

When people look at property as an investment option, they tend to ask themselves, "Can I afford this property?" However, the correct question to ask oneself is "How can I arrange for the down payment (Seed Money) and use the benefit of leverage/ O.P.M to buy that property and to keep my risks at minimum?"

SIMPLIFYING THE IDEA IN 3 EASY STEPS

Making a decision: You can buy a home worth INR 1 crore with just INR 10 lakhs in hand by opting for bank loan rarely does one find a deal where you can buy something worth INR 1 crore for INR 10 lakhs.

Implementing the decision: You just spent INR 10 lakhs and now control an asset worth one crore if your properties value goes by 5 percent that's INR 5 lakhs which is 50 percent of the money that you put in to the deal.

Reaping the fruits: If the asset value goes up 10 percent which is INR 10 lakhs or by 100 percent of the money that you invested in the property, then you have earned 100 percent return on your investment.

START SMALL: THE PERSON WHO HAD JUST
INR 50,000 FOR INVESTING IN PROPERTY

Let me give you another example of an investor, Mr. Deepak Kale, who had only a sum of INR 50,000 to invest. I advised him to buy a one-room kitchen (1RK) residential property in Thane for INR 4.5 lakhs.

On down payment of INR 50,000, he could get the loan of INR 4 lakhs. The EMI amount of the loan was around INR 4000 per month. As this was a ready property, he rented is out immediately for INR 3000 p.m. He paid the difference amount of INR 1000 p.m. from his own pocket.

The rent amount increased over the years so his contribution amount toward the EMI went on decreasing year on year basis. After a period of just 6 years, the value of the property had increased significantly from INR 4.5 lakhs to INR 12 lakhs. He then sold the property at that price and repaid outstanding bank loan, which was amounting to INR 3 lakhs. After repaying the bank loan amount, he still had around INR 9 lakhs in hand.

That is the magic of leverage! He had invested just INR 50,000 as an investment and small amounts periodically, to fill the gaps in EMI. At the end however, he had INR 9 lakhs, a large amount in hand. He made around twenty times on his investment, which is almost impossible to attain in any other investment.

"Use leverage to maximize your R.O.I."
– Amjad Khan

	Amount in lakhs
Total Value of property home/office	4.50
Amount paid as down payment including stamp duty	0.50
The amount of bank loan availed	4.00
The total amount paid toward EMI over 6 years	2.70
The amount of rent received over the year's (6 years)	2.80
Sell value of the property after 6 years	**12.00**
Less bank loan	3.00
Net amount received in hand	**9.00**

Where else can you achieve such returns?

If he had invested this INR 50,000 in Mutual Funds and that mutual fund would have given him a return of 12 percent p.a. Even then, his investment would have grown to only INR 1 lakh in six years. Just forget the gold or bank FDs where his investment would have fetched just few thousand rupees more. Therefore, nothing can beat the power of leverage to build the wealth at a fast pace. You can start with as little as INR 50,000 or INR 1 lakh to invest in properties. Don't think that you should have large amount of money to invest in properties?

"Real estate investing, even on a very
small scale, remains a tried and true
means of building an individual's
cash flow and wealth."
– Robert Kiyosaki

I can give you hundreds of examples where by using the power of leverage people have, multiplied there investment by six times in just seven years. You can calculate your own R.O.I in the property you bought by availing bank loan to see how unknowingly you have used the power of leverage to work for you. Assume you sell your self-occupied property today, what is the R.O.I that you have earned?

Total value of property home/office which you bought	
Amount paid as down payment including stamp duty etc.	
The amount of bank loan availed	
The total amount paid toward EMI over the years	
The amount of rent received over the years	
Sell value of the property	
Less outstanding amount of bank loan	
Net amount you will get in hand	

If you are residing in the property you bought, then you can calculate the expected rent you could have received, had you given out the place on rent.

From your own example, you learned how the leverage has worked for you. Just compare it with the R.O.I that you have earned out of your other forms of investments and you now know where to invest your money in future.

According to AyaLaraya,
"When you invest, you are buying
the day that you don't have to work"

WHERE SHOULD YOU INVEST
IN THE CURRENT TIMES?

If you have invested in properties specially homes in last five years then the leverage will work reverse for you, because in last couple of years the property prices have skyrocketed in all metro cities, not making it advisable to invest in homes (residential realty) in the current scenario. Instead, you can invest in offices/ warehouses/ shops (commercial realty) in current market conditions, which will give very good rental returns as well as high appreciation in the future. The supply of commercial realty is currently inelastic and demand is picking up because majority of the developers have concentrated on building more of 'Residential Reality' as compared to 'Commercial Reality' because it is easy for them to lure the innocent homebuyers. Chapter 3 helps you to make an informed choice by selecting the right property at the right time, in the right location to maximize your returns.

Other than leveraging your money, you can also use other type of leverage, to your advantage in building lasting wealth for you at a brisk pace.

OPT – Other People's Time
OPW – Other People's Work
OPE – Other People's Experience and Knowledge
OPC – Other People's Connections
OPT - Other People's Time and Work

There are many agencies and individuals that will sell you their time like laborers to professionals specialized in particular field like property agents, lawyers, consultants, property managers, finance brokers, etc. can save your time and money. You can use the free time to learn how to make more money.

OTE / OPE - Other People's Experience and Knowledge

Instead of learning, everything through trial and error and wasting lots of time and money doing that, you can leverage the experience and knowledge of other people to your advantage you can learn from their experiences, knowledge and mistakes.

OPC - Other People's Connections

Connection is important because they jump you ahead and help you to get your stalled up work speedily. If you are able to make right connections, you go to a different level altogether.

L. R. D - LEASE RENT DISCOUNTING

Lease rent discounting is metaphorically like the magical **LAMP** of Aladdin, which enables you to fulfill your big dreams and desires! It's the fastest and surest way to massive wealth creation.

WHAT IS LRD AND HOW DOES IT WORK?

Lease rent discounting (LRD) is a term loan offered against rental receipts derived from lease contracts with tenants. The rent is considered as a *Fixed Income* over a stipulated time (lease or rent period or tenure) that the borrower may earn, and he is given a loan based upon the rent to be received over the period of lease by a bank.

For example, if you are an owner of the property (office/shop) which is generating INR 1 lakh as monthly rental income and you have given the property on a lease term of ten years. Therefore, in 10 years, you will receive a total rent of INR 1.50 cr. including 5 percent escalation in the rent every year. So the bank will give you loan to the tune INR 1 cr. (60-70 percent amount of the total rental receipts), now the rent will be directly deposited with the lender (bank).

You can get around 70 percent of the amount before-hand, of the gross rent to be received by you over a period of ten years.

You can start a new business or buy another income generating property from the same amount and then you can take LRD on that property as well, to buy a third property. You can repeat this process three to four times to create a portfolio of properties from one single property. You don't need to bother about EMI's as it will be paid automatically from the rent received by the tenants. After some years if you receive good appreciation in the market you can sell any of the property and clear the loan of the rest of the properties, so that you can start receiving rental income in your hand.

"If you don't own a home, buy one. If you own a home, buy another one. If you own two homes, buy a third."
— *John Paulson*

THE MAGIC OF ALADDIN'S GENIE

The ultimate power of LRD scheme is that you get any amount to buy a pre-leased property irrespective of your own income credentials.

Let us suppose that as per your current income credentials, you are eligible for a loan amount of maximum INR 1 crore. However, if you are buying a pre-leased property, you can get a loan of INR 10 crores. Loan is given on the basis of gross rental returns property generates over the terms of the lease. Let me explain.

"Leverage is a magical genie that can realize your wildest dreams."
– Amjad Khan

Suppose you are buying a property worth INR 12 crores, which is having a R/P Ratio of 8 p.a. that means you will get a rent of INR 8 lakhs p.m. Property is leased to a corporate on a long lease period of twelve years with the escalation clause of 5 percent every year. The total rent you will receive in twelve years is INR 15.28 crores and you can get 70 percent LRD loan on that which amounts to INR 10 crores. You can arrange INR 2 crores as down payment and take LRD loan of INR 10 crores on this property.

"I like thinking big. If you're going to be thinking anything, you might as well think big."
– Donald Trump

HOW LEVERAGE WORKS IN PROPERTY INVESTMENT

PERSON - A	PERSON - B
Cost of Property **80.00 Lakh**	**Cost of Property** **20.00 Lakh**
Down Payment **(DP)** **20.00 Lakh**	Down Payment **(DP)** **20.00 Lakh**
Loan (For 10 years @10.50%) **60.00 Lakh**	**Loan** **00.00**
Total **EMI** paid **Rs. 77,000** pm x 120 months **92.04 Lakh**	**Rent** received **Rs 10,000/-** pm with 7% escalation every year **16.57 Lakh**
Total **Rent** received **Rs 40,000/-** per month with 7% escalation every year on basic Rent **66.03 Lakh**	**Value** of the Property after 10 years (Assuming 7% appreciation) **40.00 Lakh**
Difference amount paid towards **EMI** (EMI paid - Total rent received) **26.01 Lakh**	**Down Payment (DP/Net Out Flow)** **20.00 Lakh**
Value of the Property after 10 years (Assuming 7% appreciation) **1.60 Cr.**	**Net Gain : 36.57 Lakh** (Property Value + Rent - DP)
DP + EMIs Paid - Rent **46.01 Lakh**	**KEY TAKE AWAY :** While both the persons invested the same lumpsum amount. Net gain of **Person A** is three times more compared to **Person B**. Because **Person A** used the **POWER OF LEVERAGE** to his advantage and he is in much better financial position compared to **Person B**.
Net Gain : 1.13 Crore (Current value - Net Out Flow)	

I have bought a similar property wherein I am getting a R/P Ratio of 9 percent per annum. So now you know why I term LRD as "Aladdin's Magical Lamp."The biggest feature of LRD loan is that it's generally given at lower interest rate, at least 2 to 3 percent cheaper than the term loan.

Though you can get a sizeable amount as a loan due to the LRD scheme, you have to apply precautions while taking such big amount of loan, because you are taking a loan on the basis of the rental receivable over the years. If your lease defaults in payment or you evict him out of the place before time, then in that case you will have to bear the EMI's from your own pocket until you get the new lease. Therefore, if you have the capacity to arrange for the EMI amounts in such a scenario, then only you should get in to it, you have to keep a mindset that on an average for one year, your place will remain empty in *ten years time.*

So now you know how you can fast track your wealth creation by using the power of leverage. It's a phenomenal concept. You can use other forms of leverages also, to jet speed your goal achievement process. Leverage is a very effective concept and we need to use it often to speed up our aspiration achievement process.

"Invest the "Seed Money" in real estate and
watch the tree grow taller and
taller every day."
– Amjad Khan

You also understand the importance of a down payment in wealth creation. We can call it *Seed Money* because there cannot be a tree without the seed. In the following chapters, I am going to give you many ideas on how to generate seed money (down payment amount), make use of them and start the process of wealth creation for subsequent financial freedom (early retirement). "Progress happens outside of one's comfort zone", should be noted by all.

"Believe you can and you're halfway there."
– Theodore Roosevelt

Chapter 6

What Titles or Clearances Should you Check?

"Diligence is the mother of good fortune"
– Benjamin Disraeli

Due diligence is the most important factor when you buy properties, because the amount in question is colossal compared to any other investment you make. You are putting your hard-earned money to make a down payment and then you work hard for the ensuing years to manage money for the EMIs. You must therefore be extra cautious while making any investment in Real Estate. There are different titles and clearances that you need to check, while buying different types of Real estate. I am giving you a general idea of the clearances you need to check while buying different types of Real Estate but only one thing is common among all–whatever property you buy, always buy only ready possession properties. This saves us a lot of heartache in the later years and ensures that we are picking up a property that will not entangle us in legal hurdles or encumbrances that will result in years of hardships for us.

"Buying a home today is a complex process,
but that is no way it excuses home buyers from
their obligation for due diligence"
– Henry Paulson.

"Keep all your eggs in one basket, but
watch that basket closely."
– Warren Buffet

Before going further, get familiar with following important concepts:

- **C.C**: Commencement Certificate
- **O.C**: Occupation Certificate
- **A.P.F**: Approved Project Finance
- **RERA**: Real Estate Regulation Act
- **N.A.**: Non Agriculture
- **F.S.I**: Floor Space Index
- **T.D.R**: Transfer of Development Rights

C.C: COMMENCEMENT CERTIFICATE

The Local governing authorities (Municipal Corporations) issue a commencement certificate to the builder, to start the work on the plot as per the plan scrutinized and sanctioned by the authorities. After purchasing the plot or taking the development rights of the plot, the builder with the help of his architect prepares a plan (Blue Prints) of the building to be constructed on the respective plot of land. You should always insist on seeing the sanctioned plan and commencement certificate (CC) if you are buying an under construction property. You must also compare the sanctioned plan with the sale plan prepared by the builder, to see if he is doing any extra construction in the flat, compared to the sanctioned plan as this can result in difficulty in getting occupation certificate for the building.

O.C: OCCUPATION CERTIFICATE

OC means that the building is ready in all respects to occupy and enjoy. When the building is ready in all respect as per the terms mentioned in CC, the local authority checks everything. They check whether building is constructed as per the sanctioned plan or not, if the number of parking areas are provided as per norms, things like rain water harvesting system, solar water heater system has been provided as per the sanctioned plan or not. In addition, the plantation of trees/ functioning of lifts/ fire fighting system/ sewerage system, etc. will be checked by the authorities. It is when they are completely satisfied that the building is fully ready for occupation, they issue the Occupation Certificate. Therefore, while buying any ready possession apartment you must check the OC copy and the sanctioned plan copy because according to the government only after receiving an OC, the property is meant to be occupied by the occupant. This means that you can legally stay in the flat only after receiving O.C. So always buy property that is ready to occupy so that you can immediately start living in it or you can rent it out instantaneously.

F.S.I: FLOOR SPACE INDEX

F.S.I simply means the total amount of area that you can build upon a plot. Suppose you buy a 2000 sq.ft. plot of land, where the permissible F.S.I. in that area is 1:1, then you can construct a 2000 sq.ft. bungalow or building on it. If F.S.I is 0.5, then you can construct 1000 sq.ft. structure on that plot. Before buying a property, you must be aware of the F.S.I permissible on that plot. The higher the F.S.I, the larger the structure you can construct, and derive more money and value from the property.

T.D.R: TRANSFER OF DEVELOPMENT RIGHTS

The local Municipal Corporation acquires land from private property owners for constructing and expansion of civic amenities and infrastructure like roads, gardens, stadium, etc. The Transfer of Development Rights or T.D.R., is awarded in lieu of this acquired land, by giving them a certain amount of additional built up area in lieu of the area surrendered by the owner of the land. He can either use the extra built up area for himself or transfer it to another person (builder) who is in need of the extra build up area, for a handsome compensation. Suppose a landowner relinquishes an area of 5000 sq.ft. to the Local Corporation for the construction of a DP road then the Corporation issues him a T.D.R. certificate of 5000 sq.ft. He either can use that on his own balance plot of land, or can sell that certificate to any other person or builder who can construct that much area in addition to the available F.S.I. on his plot. Normally builders buy theT.D.R.to construct an additional floor in the building. In many areas, marked under Municipal Corporation / Council jurisdiction, an F.S.I. is up to 1 and the T.D.R. is up to 0.8, allowed as per the law. Therefore, if you have 1000 sq.ft. plot, you can construct 1800 (1000+800) sq.ft. area on it after buying a T.D.R. of 800 sq.ft. from another person.

RERA: REAL ESTATE REGULATION AND DEVELOPMENT ACT

This act is enacted by the Government of India to protect and safe guard the interest of the property buyers in India. Though it is applicable in many of the states across the country, it is yet to be enacted in few others. In states like Maharashtra, it is already functional. Therefore, if you are buying an under construction property (which I may not suggest in any of these states), your interests are safe guarded by the Government, provided that the developer has registered the project with RERA authorities. If the builder delays the possession of your flat, you can seek compensation by filing a complaint with the RERA authorities. I however strongly recommend that you should not buy any property that is not registered with RERA. Kindly note the RERA registration is not applicable to the projects where OC is already received.

APF: APPROVED PROJECT FINANCE

This number is issued by the bankers or financing companies who provide home loans. The APF number is provided for a particular housing project. The bank scrutinizes the necessary licenses and documents such as the title certificate, the building plan approval, and decide if the project is deemed fit for financing the homes in it. Only after satisfying themselves with all the papers, they issue a unique identification number or the APF number so that they can sanction the loan easily. The number indicates that a certain project, has been thoroughly scrutinized and has received the necessary approvals. We should always buy property in the project where the bank or the housing finance company, has issued the APF number to ensure that the property project is genuine and that the builder actually has all necessary approvals, Even if the bank scrutinizes the documents and issues an APF letter, in the end, if some legal issues crop up, the banks do not take any responsibility toward the same. They will ask you to service the loan even if the project work has stalled.

Title:

The lawyer issues the **title** certificate after scrutinizing all the documents related to the property, stating that the property has a clear and marketable title. Before you buy any property, make sure that you check its title with the advocate who will carry out the search report and issue a title certificate. It makes sense to pay a small amount, to the lawyer (@INR 10-15 K) especially when you are buying piece of land.

"If you do not like real estate, all you have to do is make hamburgers, build a business around that hamburger, and franchise it."
– Robert Kiyosaki

FINE TUNING INTO SOME MORE CONCEPTS BEFORE BUYING ANY PROPERTY:

Total Cost of the Property:

Charges like GST, Stamp Duty, Registration charges, Development Charges, parking charges, etc. can elevate the cost of the property by 5 to 20 percent. After adding these costs, you will arrive at an *all inclusive cost* of the property and then you divide this cost with the area of the property, to reach at a final per sq.ft. rate of the property. For example, if you bought at property at INR 10,000 per sq.ft. and if you add all other incidental charges, the actual per sq.ft. rate might be INR 12000 per sq.ft.; when you want to sell the property you will get consideration in lieu with the ongoing per sq.ft. rate in the area.

Total Cost of Maintenance:

This will include the maintenance charges and property tax, repair costs, etc., so that you know exactly how much you have to fork out every month toward these charges, and only after deducting all these charges, will you arrive at exact R/P Ratio (Rent to Price Ratio) of your property.

Future Maintenance:

For the future maintenance of the property, you need to make sure that the property you are buying in the complex shall be maintained properly over a long term. Check whether they have made provisions for a corpus fund to maintain the common amenities like the clubhouse, swimming pool, etc. Check whether the builder has handed over the maintenance to the housing society, and whether society members have the right frame of mind toward the maintenance of the complex. Long ago, I had bought a property in a small mall for my office, where maintenance ended up being so bad that finally I had to sell the place, and shift my office to another office building.

Find Average Price Range:

The average price range in the locality should be known, to make sure that you are buying the property at fair market value going around that area. The rates may vary to a smaller extent within the vicinity (10-20 percent) depending upon the factors like quality of construction, amenities provided, configuration of the properties, etc.

Know your builder:

If you are buying an under construction property, you should look at the past performance of the builder, and verify whether he has delivered the previous project on time, check the quality delivered by him to assume that it would be same quality he would deliver for you too.

Loan Amount:

If you are a buying property on loan, make sure that you are getting the best rate of interest because a near 0.5 percent higher rate of interest, could result in you shelling out a much higher amount toward interest payment in the long term. Suppose you have taken a loan of INR 1 crore for a fifteen year tenure, to buy a property and have paid 0.5 percent higher interest rate, you will end up paying INR 5 lakhs more toward servicing the same. I suggest that you take the services of the loan broker or apply to a few different banks to draw a great bargain and get the best possible interest rate with a minimum down payment amount.

So before you buy any property kindly check all these things before arriving at purchase decision:

- Sanction Plan Copy – Blueprints
- CC – Commencement Certificate
- OC – Occupation Certificate
- APF – Letter from Bank
- Title Certificate from advocate
- N.A order, N.A Tax paid receipt
- All inclusive cost of the property
- Total outgo toward maintenance & property tax
- Smooth long term maintenance provisions
- Fair market value of the property

"Everyone wants a piece of land. It's the only sure investment. It can never depreciate like a car or washing machine. Land will only double its value in ten years."
– Sam Sheppard

WHAT YOU SHOULD KNOW IF YOU ARE BUYING AN N. A. PLOT OR WEEKEND BUNGALOWS

If you are buying an N.A. plot or weekend home, the first thing you should look for, is the maintenance provision and after sales service offered by the developer. Generally, most of the developers of such projects sell the last plot or bungalow and get out of the project by handing over common society maintenance to the members. As many of the investors buy N.A. plots for investment purposes and are hardly able to visit the project occasionally, maintaining the common amenities becomes a challenge for them. Besides, many members do not pay their maintenance dues on time and since they are residing across different locations in the city, it become impossible for the Managing Committee to collect monthly maintenance from them.

"I have always liked real estate; farm land, pasture land, timber land and city property. I have had experience with all of them. I guess I just naturally like 'the good Earth,' the foundation of all our wealth."
– Jesse Jones

Gradually due to the paucity of funds, the project maintenance deteriorates and finally it reaches a point where whole maintenance system falls apart. I have seen many such projects where there is no maintenance work being carried out; there is no security at the main gate, no electricity and no regular water supply and no one to trim the grass that may have grown to height of 8-10 feet all over the project. The people who bought these plots and bungalows with different dreams in mind, repent their decision because instead of getting appreciation, the value of their investment starts declining.

Therefore, if you are buying any N.A. plot or bungalow you should confirm on prior basis if the developer has made any provision of corpus fund to take care of the maintenance of the project on a long-term basis.

Corpus fund is nothing but a one-time amount collected by the developer from all the plot or bungalow owners to create a sizeable corpus fund so that the maintenance of the common amenities can be taken care of, from the interest amount generated out of the corpus fund amount every month. The builder then transfers this amount to the society and the society members can easily make payments of common utility bills from the corpus fund.

Greenery is a part of the corpus fund provision and an important part of the N.A. plot projects. You should check on whether the developer has provided quality infrastructure and amenities. Also, check whether he has planted enough saplings to insure a green canopy for the future. Greenery appreciates the value of the project because more people seek peace and tranquility and they willingly pay a higher value for the same N.A. plots or bungalows as compared to other similar projects where greenery is scarce.

The following important papers, you should cross check before buying any N.A. plot or weekend bungalow:

- 7/12 extract of the particular plot you want to buy.
- Sanction plan copy of the plot / bungalow layout.

- N.A. order issued by the tahsildar/collector.
- Survey map of the plot you are buying issued by local T.I.L.R.
- Title certificate issued by the advocate.
- APF latter issued by the bank and financial institutes.
- Yearly out go amount toward plot/bungalow.
- Safety of your plot/bungalow.
- Accessibility to local market.
- Approachability to the place.
- Future appreciation prospects of the project and local area.

ADDITIONAL POINTERS

1: Can you get Rental Income from your weekend bungalow?
Yes, you can. You can also check whether the developer has any provision of getting rental returns to its bungalow owner, wherein you can enjoy your weekend as per your convenience and can rent out the place on some of the days when you're not visiting the place as rental income can be helpful in paying the part of the EMI. Those developers who have such provisions, maintain the project nicely for their own interest.

"Landlords grow rich in their sleep."
– John Stuart Mill

2: Follow due diligence before investing:
In case of any real estate investments there is a very big amount at stake so kindly follow due diligence before investing in any kind

of property. Please take personal advice from friends or relatives and take professional advice from your advocate, architect, property consultants, property coaches, etc. Do not shy away from visiting the place twice or thrice at different times of the day. Ask the current residents whether they are facing any issues related to the water supply, electricity, common maintenance, etc. You can also ask the previous customers about their experience of the developer. Please don't shy away from visiting the concerned government office if you need clarity on any issue, in short make sure that you are making an informed decision.

Chapter 7

How to Organize the Down Payment?

"Many folk think that they are not good with money, when what they don't know is how to use it."
– Frank Clark, American Footballer

Through this book, I have suggested ways to use the power of leverage to buy properties. The fastest way to use this idea is when you buy an INR 1 crore property with INR 25 lakhs as a down payment, which on appreciation will become an INR 2 crore property in the next five to ten years. Let us suppose you do not have the adequate liquidity to sponsor your down payment.

You can follow the following options to arrange the same:

- Liquidating gold / Taking a loan against gold
- Sell underperforming properties
- Loan against FD's / MF's/ NSC/ LIC Policy
- Selling off the non performing / Unused assets
- Short time mortgage against existing home / Top up loan against existing home loan
- Loans from friends and family
- Withdrawing your Provident Fund/ Taking loan from your company/ Employees Society
- Proprietors and MSME owners can avail Over Draft Facility
- Negotiating with the bank for a 90 percent loan
- Request the builder to make an all inclusive agreement to reduce the down payment
- Take the LRD loan against your leased commercial property

I am explaining in this chapter how you can apply any of these strategies to arrange for the down payment you will need to buy a property. However, I am again stressing the need to purchase a ready property so your risks are minimized.

"If you buy things you do not need, soon you will have to sell things you need."
– Warren Buffett

LIQUIDATING GOLD / TAKING A
LOAN AGAINST GOLD:

Liquidating gold or taking a loan against gold is one of the fastest methods of generating cash, without having to create additional paper work. You can liquidate the gold owned by your family to generate funds. If they are reluctant to part with their ornaments permanently, you can also approach organizations that offer a loan against gold at attractive rates. Today, all leading banks and companies like Muhthoot or Mallapuram Finance offer loan against gold at 10.5 percent and up to 75 percent of the value of the gold you pledge.

SELLING OFF THE UNDERPERFORMING ASSETS:

You may have a piece of land in the village or a flat that is not getting returns. You may also have a property, which falls under Poor Property as per my Property Measurement Matrix, then you can sell it and pay that amount toward buying an excellent property. You can call this process "Portfolio Makeover."

LOAN AGAINST FDS / MFS/ NSC/ LIC POLICY

As we have seen in the earlier chapters, Indians are prone to holding a significant part of their savings in the above-mentioned instruments. Traditionally, there is no Indian family that would not hold a few FDs, LIC policies, a few thousands rupees worth National Savings Certificates. The collective worth of these investments may run in to a few lakh rupees in most families.

The jet setting generation however is savvier in their approach to investments and their portfolio will definitely reflect a major chunk of finances kept aside in Liquid Funds. Incase this is absent; you can always take a loan against the current value of your NSC/ MF or FDs, Equities and your Life Policies. This is another hassle free way of obtaining funds without liquidating your investments.

SELLING OFF THE NON PERFORMING / UNUSED ASSETS:

We all have a record of making some purchases that have ended up being more of a liability than an asset. These acquisitions like an expensive, fancy car / bike of foreign make, a vintage vehicle, designer watches or cell phones are mere life style statements. These decisions are driven by their brand value than our needs. We may also have invested more than one car for our family. If the entire family can manage with one family car, the other vehicle can be sold off to raise funds. We may also have some antiques or collector's paintings, murals and sculptures, which may have been acquired in jest or have been in the family for generations. At such moments, we must keep our emotions aside and drive a hard bargain for these collector items we have amassed. The cash garnered from the sale of antiques and collector's items can be a fine surprise for many! If needed, seek professional help in determining their value and their sale. We can sell these unused assets or non-performing assets to raise the amount needed for down payment.

"Most people think small because most people are afraid of success, afraid of making decisions, afraid of winning. And that gives people like me a great advantage."
– *Donald Trump*

LOAN AGAINST PROPERTY / TOP UP LOAN ON YOUR HOME LOAN ACCOUNT:

1- Mortgage against property - The down payment amount you need is much less compared to current value of your flat so the bank is more than willing to consider your case. The risk you take is very moderate when you buy a ready property, you start earning rent immediately.

2- Top-Up against current home loan account - As your home loan is already sanctioned, the bank will consider your case positively when you apply for a Top-Up loan. As you have repaid a sizeable amount of principal and interest on this loan, this idea can help you generate the down payment in a shorter duration.

LOANS FROM FRIENDS AND FAMILY:

In suggesting ways and means of raising loans, I will take the liberty of suggesting that you can also approach your friends and family for loans. We do have some friends and family members who are financially well placed. In case of a short fall, you can always take a tide over loan from them and repay it with interest so that the person does not miss appreciation of his funds. In addition, it keeps your relations on a clear understanding. Maybe even your parents can spare some retirement funds if you return them diligently. The edge is that you may not be asked for a collateral security, and there is no fixed EMI to repay the loan. This flexibility is a cushion enjoyed only with family and friends and thus it eases the tension of repayment.

WITHDRAWING YOUR PROVIDENT FUNDS / TAKING A LOAN FROM YOUR COMPANY/ EMPLOYEES SOCIETY:

Many persons have ample funds accumulated in their PF fund accounts for utilization of a major expense like the child's fees, or marriage or as their retirement corpus. If retirement or any of the above expenses are not in the immediate future, then you can also look at your funds in the **PF or EPF or PPF,** to raise the down payment amounts. One need not look at any other avenue, when you use this method to create a source of cash flow. Also, look at the positive side to it.

PROPRIETORS AND MSME OWNERS CAN AVAIL OVER DRAFT FACILITY:

SME and MSME owners are not new to the concept of Business OD, neither are they averse to the idea. They are provided against your assets for a fixed period or a rolling facility and can be secured or unsecured in nature. Most entrepreneurs will have an OD created for their business, which is secured and authorized and they can avail of it when the down payment needs to be organized. If your OD is pre-sanctioned and authorized, you will save on the cost of arranging the money, legal and facilitation fees too. You need to take bank's permission before utilizing OD facility for down payment.

NEGOTIATING WITH THE BANK
FOR A 90 PERCENT LOAN:

The Real Estate industry is a fast changing one, and most developers are slowly and surely moving from their previous grey nature to a much transparent and customer centric business module. Also in this highly competitive market, the customers are spoilt for a choice as construction industry grows rapidly. As we are all aware, it is the client's responsibility to organize funds and to bear the *additional costs* like stamp duty and registration, parking charges levied by the developer, GST and development and other charges claimed by the builder in his agreement. These funds may well run into 10 to 20 percent of the value of your flat or office. This means it is an added effort to consolidate our funds.

Let us suppose you are buying a property worth INR 50 lakhs. You will need to make a down payment of INR 8 lakhs initially, and there will be additional charges of INR 10 lakhs as mentioned in the above paragraph. On an agreement value of INR 40 lakhs, your bank will sanction a home loan to the tune of 80 percent, which is INR 32 lakhs. Moreover, all the above mentioned expenses will be shelled out of your pocket (stamp duty and registration, parking charges levied by the developer, GST and development and other charges).This means you have to make an arrangement of INR 18 lakhs for buying a property of INR 50 lakhs.

Now consider this option, today the developers are keen to help the clients by offering some alternatives. If you negotiate with you developer, he will create an *All Inclusive Agreement* of INR 50 lakhs for your property, including all the additional costs mentioned above. On an agreement value of INR 50 lakhs, the bank will offer 80 percent home loan that translates to INR 40 lakhs, some bank can offer loan up to 90 percent. Which means you will have to pay only 5 to 10 lakhs as down payment. Negotiate with different banks for higher loans (up to 90 percent) which will translate in to lower down payment on your part.

L.R.D LOAN:

You can take L.R.D loan against the commercial property that you have leased. Suppose you have a commercial property that gives you a rent of INR 1 lakhs per month and you have leased it out for a period of five years, then your total rent amount for five years will be INR 60 lakhs and against this rent, you can avail L.R.D of 70-80 percent. This will give you a tidy sum for making the down payment.

I have tapped upon several avenues of raising down payment, some conventional and some unconventional. As stated by Virgil, *"fortune sides with him who dares."* To achieve your goals you need to shift your gears and move out of your comfort zone. The one who pushes the envelope, sees the results. To create down payments for your dream property you must try the above initiatives:

- Look closer to your home for funds
- Tap every unconventional resource for fund generation
- Don't be emotionally swayed when taking financial decisions
- Look at the larger picture and ignore short term discomfort
- Squeeze out the best deal for yourself and never feel shy of negotiating
- Seek professional help where relevant, as it may actually get you the best deal

Chapter 8

Commercial Property v/s Residential Property - An Engaging Viewpoint

---

"Twenty years from now, you will be disappointed with the things you didn't do than by the things you did"
– Mark Twain

Your home is not an investment but a liability, because you are never going to sell it and realize its value in cash. You are not getting any cash flow dividends from it, instead, you are spending money to maintain it.

"Rule #1: You must know the difference between an asset and a liability, and buy assets. If you want to be rich, this is all you need to know. It is rule number one. It is the only rule. This may sound absurdly simple, but most people have no idea how profound this rule is. Most people struggle financially because they do not know the difference between an asset and a liability. Rich people acquire assets. The poor and middle class acquire liabilities that they think are assets, said rich dad."
– Robert Kiyosaki

One of the major chunks of our investment goes toward buying a home. We spend 50 percent of our monthly earning on servicing the EMIs, and it takes around 2/3rd of our working life to repay the EMI. We think it is our basic need and we need (which can be fulfilled by renting a place) to buy it regardless of the price. Since it is an emotional decision, we invest in it without running the numbers, we forget about calculating the return on investment and that is probably the chief reason of the current underperformance of housing Real Estate market in India. Make sure that the home you buy has a real potential to increase in value, enough to make it a sound investment.

"The problem is that most people think of home values as Real Estate as a whole. Homes make terrible investments and shouldn't be looked at when deciding what the Real Estate market is doing. The key to real estate investment is its ability to produce cash flow (i.e. dividend – rental income). Single family homes do not create cash flow for investor, so they are not investment." - By Eric Bowling, Financial Express, 12/11/17.

Your house is not an asset, it is a liability
– Robert Kiyosaki

The house that we buy with the intention of self-occupation should be treated as a liability and not as an asset. Kiyosaki has emphasized that as investors we make a blind evaluation of our self-occupied property as an asset. We tend to forget that it is never an avenue of cash flow for us and on top of it, we spend thousands of rupees on the maintenance and upkeep of this property. So, consider it as a liability, as it generates no income for us.

MAKE A WISE CHOICE, INVEST IN
COMMERCIAL PROPERTY

Looking at the current Real Estate market, it makes perfect financial sense to buy commercial Real Estate as compared to residential property. Because most of the developers are concentrating on constructing residential properties, the supply of residential properties is accelerated in the market, but the demand is stagnant. According to a Knight Franks report, there is an unsold inventory of thousands of flats in each metro city of India, which will take years to get sold. While there is no dearth in supply of 'Quality Residential Projects', there is a deficit of 'Quality Commercial Office Spaces' in India. We need Commercial buildings or complexes offering lifestyle amenities that one sees in residential projects. For example- Designer entrance lobbies, excellent landscaping, superior finishes and common amenities like a good restaurant or canteen, ample parking spaces, etc. People seek similar amenities in offices (working spaces) as they get in modern residential projects.

There is a healthy demand for quality commercial office spaces/ quality industrial parks/ warehouses/ retail spaces and malls across India. There is also an equal and urgent need for individuals to harvest the benefits through investments in commercial realty spaces. The investors need to come out of their comfort zone and shed the idea of purchasing a second home in a far off suburb, as an investment. They need to look at commercial properties as a lucrative investment procuring higher returns. They need to study the stability of returns in this sector, the stupendous appreciation in ten years and use the power of leverage to build a portfolio of properties, to generate massive passive income for themselves.

Let me explain with two examples:

- Person **A** bought Commercial property of INR 1 crore making a DP of INR 25 lakhs and taking a loan of INR 75 lakhs at 10 percent interest rate for tenure of fifteen years. His EMI will work out to INR 82,905.
- He then rented out that property at an R/P ratio of 6 percent, earning a rental of INR 50,000 with a Y-O-Y escalation of 5 percent in rental income every year.
- At the EMI of INR 82,905 x 180 months, he paid a total loan amount of INR 1.50 crores.
- However, against this he had already earned a rent of INR 1.30 crores, making his total outgo only INR 20 lakhs (Total EMI – Total Rent).
- The current value of his property assuming 8 percent appreciation every year is INR 3.17 crores and after considering his Net outflow of INR 45 lakhs (DP+ EMI - Rent), his Net Gain is INR 2.72 crores.
- In 15 years his loan is repaid and he become owner of a property worth 3.17 crores which is generating rental income of INR 1,58,500 at R/P ratio of 6 percent.
- Person **B** bought Residential property of INR 1 crore making a DP of INR 25 lakhs and taking a loan of INR 75 lakhs at 8.7 percent interest rate for tenure of fifteen years. His EMI will work out to INR 74,737.
- He then rented out that property at an R/P ratio of 2.4 percent, earning a rental of INR 20,000 with a Y-O-Y escalation of 5 percent in rental income every year.

- At the EMI of INR 74,737 x 180 months, he paid a total loan amount of INR 1.35 crores.
- But against this he had already earned a rent of INR 52 lakhs, making his total outgo INR 83 lakhs (Total EMI – Total Rent).
- The current value of his property is INR 2.08 crores and after considering his Net outflow of INR 108 lakhs (DP + EMI - Rent), his Net Gain is INR 1 crore.

The examples have been illustrated below in a simple manner to help you realize how buying a commercial property helps to build wealth much faster than a residential property.

RECOGNIZE THE EDGE OF YOUR INVESTMENT IN A COMMERCIAL PROPERTY

Long-term investment in property has always reaped rich dividends, but commercial properties perform even better when it comes to returns. You need to look at these pointers to analyze why investing in commercial properties makes the perfect sense.

Longer Lease Period and Higher Rent: Commercial properties have longer lease periods and effectively give you a higher rental yield of 6-10 percent. While in case of residential property you get 2-3 percent of rental yield plus you have the headache to change the leasee every 11 months.

RESIDENTIAL VS COMMERCIAL PROPERTY RETURNS

Commercial Property	Residential Property
Person A buys a **1.00 Cr. Commercial Property** with a Down Payment of Rs. 25 Lakh and **Rs. 75 Lakh Loan** at 10% for 15 years **EMI is Rs. 82,905/-** He also Rents out the Property at **R/P Ratio of 6%.** He will get an amount of **Rs. 50,000/- pm** with **5%** escalation in Rent every year **(Y-O-Y)**	Person B buys a **1.00 Cr. Residential Property** with a Down Payment of Rs. 25 Lakh and **Rs. 75 Lakh Loan** at 8.7% for 15 years **EMI is Rs. 74,737/-** He Rents out the Property at **R/P Ratio of 2.4%.** His Rent is **Rs. 20,000/- pm** with **5%** escalation in Rent every year **(Y-O-Y)**
Down Payment (DP) **Rs. 25 Lakh**	**Down Payment (DP)** **Rs. 25 Lakh**
Total Loan amount repaid (EMI Rs. 82,950 pm x 180 months) **Rs. 1.50 Cr.**	**Total Loan amount repaid** (EMI Rs. 74,737 pm x 180 months) **Rs. 1.35 Cr.**
Total Rent received in 15 years **Rs. 1.30 Cr.**	**Total Rent** received in 15 years **Rs. 52.00 Lakh**
Difference amount paid towards EMI (Total EMI - Total Rent) **Rs. 20.00 Lakh**	Net outflow towards EMI (Total EMI - Total Rent) **Rs. 83.00 Lakh**
Value of the Property after 15 years at 8% appreciation Y-O-Y **Rs. 3.17 Cr.**	**Value of the Property** after 15 years at 5% appreciation Y-O-Y **Rs. 2.08 Cr.**
Net Outflow (DP + EMI - Rent) **Rs. 45 Lakh**	**Net Outflow** (DP + EMI - Rent) **Rs. 108 Lakh**
NET GAIN (Total Value - Net outflow) **Rs. 2.72 Cr.**	**NET GAIN** **Rs. 1.00 Cr.** (Total Value - Net outflow)

KEY TAKE AWAY :

- You get more Rent and cost appreciation in Commercial Property even though both the persons paid the same initial amount (DP).
- The **Person B** paid more money towards EMI because he got less rent. So his net outflow (Net investment in Property) increased.
- Also at the end of 15 years he will get 2 times lesser amount compared to P**erson A** be**c**ause appreciation in Residential Property is less compared to Commercial Property.
- **Person A** multiplied his investment 6 times, while Person B multiplied it by 2 times. So Commerci Property is faster wealth builder compared to Residential Property.

Limited Use: In commercial properties, the tenant is generally responsible for repair and upkeep. Since he is doing business in the property, he maintains the property in an excellent form. In the case of residential property, it's the landlord's responsibility and one can get a midnight call because a tenant wants some urgent repair or has lost a key. Commercial Offices / Shops are normally closed at night because tenants of commercial properties are generally companies, llc, partnership firms. Additionally, once their set up is done in the property they will not want to move out early, as their livelihood is dependent on the business. Therefore, you can let out these properties on a long lease.

"I knew if I was patient and kept
my eyes open; a better opportunity
would eventually arise."
– Donald Trump

Professional Relationship: Business owners take pride in their business and so operate peacefully and take care of the property as a part of their business. The property owner and their tenants share a cordial business-to-business customer relationship, which helps to keep the interactions professional and courteous.

Value: Retail space/ office space tenants maintain the place in an excellent form since their business is dependent on it. Sometimes you get a tenant who furnishes the place very nicely at his own expense to carry out his business. When this tenant moves out, you get a fully furnished office to let it out to another business owner for a higher rent. Good maintenance augments the life of the property and helps the owner get more value for their investment.

You are fully aware of the dismal maintenance scenario when it comes to residential tenants. Since they just use the place for staying purpose and for a shorter period, they usually don't bother much about maintenance of that place. They use the property 24x7 and if there are children, you can expect more wear and tear of a residential property. After evicting the tenant, usually you have to apply fresh coat of paint and do some minor repairs before you can hand it over to another tenant. Apart from that, the décor may also need retouching. In fact, more efforts are expected from your side in leasing and maintaining a residential property besides having good skills in managing residential tenants.

Bigger Initial Investment: Acquiring a commercial property typically requires more capital up front than acquiring the residential property. Usually you get loan up to 90 percent to purchase residential property. However, in case of commercial property you get a maximum loan of 70-80 percent. This means you have to arrange more money as down payment to buy commercial property. Thereafter you also need to have a budget provision for furnishing the commercial property because generally furnished properties get leased instantaneously. You also get higher rent, which helps you to recover your expenses made toward furniture within a period of five years. So do your own math before investing in any property using the calculator given by me, and by applying the property evaluation matrix given at the end of chapter 3. You can retain the investment that can fetch you the highest R.O.I on your seed money.

Investing in commercial real estate is not as difficult as it appears. It's just public know-how on this matter that is poor. Secondly, residential property is easier to understand to for a common man, because they can ascertain its value through comparisons which may not be so easy in commercial segment. However, they seem to miss the most crucial point here that commercial segment can generate massive R.O.I. as we can see from the comparison given below:

"Real estate is an imperishable asset, ever increasing in value. It is the most solid security that human ingenuity had devised. It is the bases of all security and about the only indestructible security."
– Russel Sage

Residential Versus Commercial Properties: Pros & Cons

THE PROS AND CONS OF BUYING
A RESIDENTIAL VS A COMMERCIAL PROPERTY

RESIDENTIAL	COMMERCIAL
Rental Income to the tune of **1 to 4%** (R/P Ratio) Rent to Price Ratio	Rental Income of **5 to 10%** (R/P Ratio) Rent to Price Ratio
Slower Appreciation of Property due to high availability, a moderate appreciation in affordable segment	**Greater Appreciation of Property** in future due to shortage in supply of Quality Commercial Real Estate
Availability of **Tax Benefits**	No **Tax Benefits**
Loan available upto **90%** Less Down Payment required	**Loan** available upto **70 to 80%** more Down Payment required
Short term of **Lease** generally **11 months**	Long term of **Lease** generally **3 to 12 years**
Regular Maintenance and **Repair** of the house is done by owner	**Maintenance** and **Upkeepment** is done normally by the **leasee**

KEY TAKE AWAY :

Commercial Properties have higher chances of appreciation. In future you also get higher rental income. It requires less effort on your part to maintain Commercial Property in the long term.

Chapter 9

Furnishing and how it Adds Value to Your Property

"Know what you own and why you own it"
– Peter Lynch

When you are talking about real estate, furnishing the residential and commercial space is an important factor as it strengthens the value of your property. Furnishing is important in the fast moving world because everyone wants ready to move in spaces. No one wants to wait and waste time and money. People are willing to pay more if the house or office being rented is semi/ fully furnished. This is because we can commence our business from there instantaneously. If you offer furnished spaces, the chances of your property getting occupied faster are more, compared to the unfurnished one. I have observed this, when the office space I wanted to give on rent didn't fetch me a client for six months because it was bare. As I began furnishing it, that space was lapped up even before the work was completed, and the best part is that I got 25 percent higher rent than my expectations. So furnishing is important because-

- It adds value to your property.
- You get 10 to 30 percent higher rent compared to a bare space.
- Your vacancy risk is minimized because it will get occupied fast.
- Your property enjoys a better occupancy ratio compared to an unfurnished one.

However, furnishing an apartment or an office is a combination of hardnosed budgeting and some practical applications. We need not compromise on quality over quantity. We must be vigilant while purchasing main furniture items like a sofa, bed and wardrobes. We can however cut few pennies on side stands, dressing tables and maybe even a dining table in an apartment. Similarly, in commercial spaces, we need to make wise decisions on work stations, filing cabinets, executive and director's desks but we can be prudent with electrical décor, flamboyant lobbies and high-end air conditioning. In addition, functionality and future maintenance by the tenant must also be considered before taking decisions.

So how does one go about it? How much should we invest in furnishing a particular property? Moreover, the main question in our mind should be– how can I do it as I don't have any past experience of doing it? In following pages, I will give you some ideas, which will be helpful for you. We will understand about three aspects of furnishing.

- Working out a budget
- Finalizing an Interior Architect
- Raising Funds for furnishing

"We don't have to be smarter than the rest. We have to be more disciplined than the rest".
– Warren Buffett

WORKING OUT A BUDGET:

Ideally, the formula to calculate your furnishing budget should be used in the following manner.

Escalated Rent Amount x 60 months = Furnishing Budget
First and foremost, what you need to decide while furnishing a place is, to arrive at a budget. How much should you spend on furnishing? Generally after furnishing the place, you earn 10 to 30 percent escalated rent, so be sure of how much additional rent you are likely to get after furnishing that place and decide the budget accordingly.

Example 1- If you own a office space and you get INR1 lakh as monthly rent and after furnishing it nicely, you expect to get INR 1.25 lakhs monthly rent, then your furnishing formula is INR 25,000 (escalated rent amount) X 60 months (five years) = INR 15,00,000 (furnishing budget). Therefore, your maximum budget for furnishing that office space should be INR 15 lakhs and you should give that budget to your interior designer, who should be an expert in office interiors.

Example 2- If you own a residential space (1 BHK) and normally you get INR 10,000 rent per month but upon furnishing it, you can expect a monthly rental of INR 12,500 then your budget for furnishing the same should be INR 1.50 lakhs. This according to my formula works as INR 2500 (escalated rent amount) X 60 months (five years rent) = INR 1.50 lakhs (furnishing budget) so how should you furnish the 1BHK space with that budget?

"If you want to sell a car and you spend five dollars to wash and polish it and then apply a little extra elbow grease, suddenly you find you can charge an extra four hundred dollars and get it."
– Donald Trump

How to use your allocated budget?

My sincere advice to you, is to buy all readymade furniture. If you employ carpenters to do it, it will consume more time, money and energy on your part to get it ready on a deadline; and the more time you are expending in finishing the task, the more rental income you will be passing up! You will also incur incidental costs toward it. Your sole purpose of furnishing the property is to give a place on rent, so the furniture should be minimal as per the requirement of the tenant, not as per the fanciful aspirations of the owner be aware of the fact you are not going to stay in it. So how do you go about managing it all within the allocated budget of INR 1.5 lakhs? I am giving you an example of itemized budget based on prevailing market rates so that you will get a fair idea on how to fit furnishing within your pre determined budget.

FURNISHING A RESIDENTIAL 1 BHK PROPERTY WITHIN THE BUDGET OF INR 1.5 LAKHS

Room wise Furniture Packages	Itemized Rate
Living Room: Sofa + Center Table	INR 25,000
Dining Area: Small TV Unit + Dining Table	INR 25,000
Bedroom: Master Bed + Side table + 2 door Wardrobe	INR 50,000
Kitchen: Trolleys (Only under the main platform)	INR 25,000
Miscellaneous: Fans + Tube light + Misc	INR 25,000
Total	**INR 1, 50,000**

FINALIZING AN INTERIOR ARCHITECT

"Simplicity is the ultimate sophistication."
– Leonardo Da Vinci

In the above paragraph, I have stressed the need to allot a budget to furnish your residential or commercial property, and how you can achieve your goal if you buy ready packages for your house, as well as the percentage of your budget you should spend on doing up an office space. However, I would also like to help you in addressing the basic question - How to select the right interior decorator, and how to deal with them?

It is important that we never lose focus that we are decorating an apartment or an office that we are not occupying as owners. Therefore fanciful ideas, expensive artifacts and high maintenance decor should be strictly avoided. We must furnish our property in a simple yet elegant manner and for that, we need a professional Interior architect.

Interior designing is an extremely niche job today and here is a step by step guide to ensure that you stay on track:

STEP BY STEP GUIDE FOR SELECTING A CONTRACTOR FOR YOUR COMMERCIAL PROPERTY

1. The first thing you should do is select a domain specific interior designer. For instance, if you are furnishing an office space, then you must select the interior decorator/ architect who specialize in office interiors.

2. You must check the earlier office spaces done by him, talk to those clients about their experience with the concerned architect. Ask if his service was up to the mark, and whether he overshot the budget?

3. Give a specific figure of your final budget and take quotations from a few individual architects or design firms and give a work order only after deciding the right person, who is ready to work as per your budget and deadlines.

4. Solemnize the deal in a written contract, stating the things to be done by him as per the given quotation,

along with the time frame and a penalty clause for missing deadlines.

5. Always award the entire contract to one single contractor. Please don't take any responsibility on yourself. Tell him specifically that you would hand over the keys of empty space to him, and within a specific period, he has to complete everything as per the given quotation (including electrical work, A/C ducting work, furniture fixture, etc.). If he delays the work beyond the given time period, he will bear the penalty on a per day basis on the delayed term. If he agrees on these terms then only award the contract to him.

6. Another due diligence should be to keep retention money of 5-10 percent of the contract value. Hire a contractor who is willing to keep the retention money because in case of any damage, breakdown or malfunction, you can demand that the contractor to do the maintenance without shelling out additional costs. It binds the contractor to give you service until your retention clause is valid. This also gives you peace of mind, if your tenant is demanding some minor repairs and maintenance regularly.

STEP BY STEP GUIDE FOR SELECTING SOURCES FOR YOUR RESIDENTIAL PROPERTY

1. In case of rental residential space, it makes sense to buy readymade furniture to furnish the house. In case of your personal residential space, you can furnish the

place as per your budget and taste, but beware of the final cost because it may escalate as the work progresses.

2. If you decide to hire a contractor, first select the right contractor after seeking a few quotations, take the quotation in writing. Take a revised quotation for every additional assignment that you give him.

3. Do your own research by comparing the prices prevailing in many areas. Sometimes, there are hubs outside city areas, which will enable you to purchase furniture at much more competitive rates than the furniture showrooms in your neighborhood. Therefore, it makes sense to visit such areas before you purchase ready furniture for your flats. For e.g. IKEA stores have come up in major cities of India. Bhiwandi or Ulhasnagar on the outskirts of Mumbai city, are furniture hubs where you can pick up ready furniture for every room, within your budget.

4. Normally it takes INR 1200-2000 on built up area to furnish the office space and INR 1000 to 4000 per sq.ft. to furnish a residential flat meant for self use. While giving your flat on rental however, you must use the formula stated in the earlier paragraphs.

RAISING FUNDS FOR FURNISHING:

"Behind every attractive room there
should be a reason."
– Unknown

Arrangement of funds is the biggest dilemma for an investor, who is furnishing the apartment or office before he gives it out on lease. As we have seen in this chapter, a semi furnished apartment/office fetches customers very easily. We can look at ways and means of raising funds for furnishing. The most brisk ways, to raise funds are:

- To take a home improvement loan
- To utilize the deposit amount accepted against the long-term lease
- To take a personal loan
- To use any of my earlier options(mentioned in the chapter seven)

To take a home improvement loan:
Home improvement loans can be procured in three formats:

One is against the mortgage of your existing home

Second is given as a top up against your existing home loans

Third is to apply for a pure home improvement loan

To utilize the deposit amount accepted against the long-term lease:
As suggested throughout this book, you must pick up a property, which is ready. You can put it up on lease immediately upon furnishing it. A fully furnished property fetches handsome rentals (10–30 percent more than an unfurnished property) and a deposit amount equivalent to six months' rent. If your commercial property is leased for a period of five years on a rent of INR 1.25

lakhs then your deposit amount would be INR 7.5 lakhs. You can temporarily use this amount for completing your furnishing work. As the lease is long term, you do not have to return the deposit amount within a year.

To take a personal loan/ credit card loan:
If you have no avenues to raise funds immediately, one alternative is to opt for a personal loan. This type of loan is sanctioned very fast and can help your project to take off. If you have a decent credit limit on your credit card, you can use this option too. However, both types of loans are interest heavy and not advisable, as the first preference. You can consider this recourse, in case you are running against time and are in urgent needs of funds. This will enable you to kick-start your work, until further arrangements are made.

To use any of my earlier options, look at the chapter seven. In that chapter, we have already touched upon several avenues to raise funds in detail, so I suggest that you look up those options once again.

The crux of the matter is to be planned and execute your budget diligently, to furnish your apartments or offices and put them on lease as early as possible, so that your rental income begins quickly. Points to imbibe:

- Decide on your budget and stick to it
- Give all work to a single contractor on a turnkey basis
- Negotiate and play quotations
- Check the previous assignments of the contractor you are hiring

- Talk to his clients to check his credentials
- Give the contractor a fixed time schedule
- Don't make changes to the contract once all items are decided
- If you make changes, take a revised quotation and file it, as you will need it for final settlement
- Keep 5-10 percent retention money to cover future problems

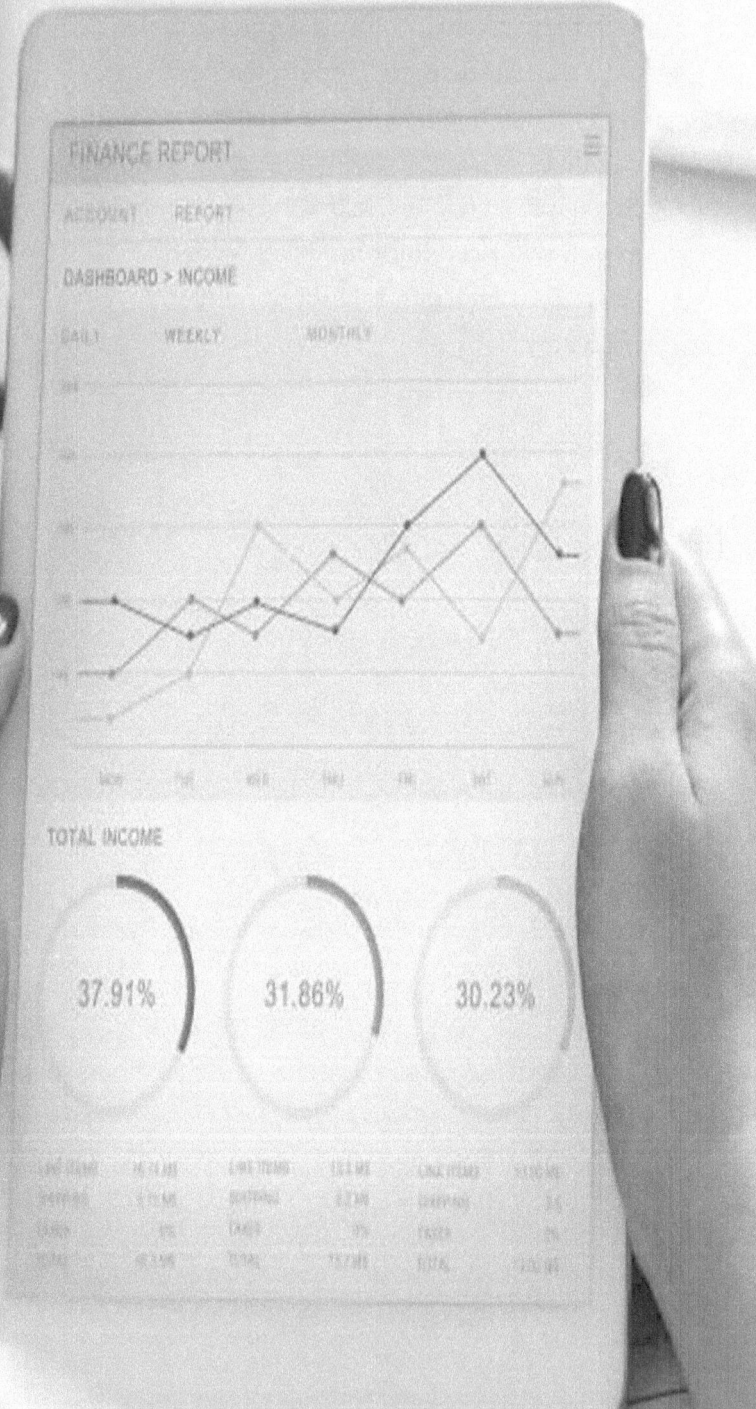

Chapter 10

Sip in Real Estate – A New Age Strategy

"The best time to plant a tree was 20 years ago. The second best time to plant a tree is today"
– Chinese Proverb

Warren Buffet has famously stated, "Someone is sitting in the shade today because someone had planted a tree long ago." Who can describe investor behavior better than the Guru of all Financial Gyaan? We have all pored over the wisdom given by these wizards of the financial world, and attempted to mimic their behavior in our investment strategy.

Who amongst us has not heard of SIPs? We are bombarded from all directions about the wisdom to start SIPs in Mutual Funds so that we accumulate a small fortune for our families by the time we retire. We make small savings every month and invest that amount in SIPs for meeting our long-term financial goals. The idea behind taking the SIP route is to create a large corpus within a certain number of years to meet our financial objectives like the higher education of our children or creating a large retirement corpus.

The basic problem with SIP is *Investor Behavior.* A large majority of people cannot stick to SIPs for the long term and usually pre-withdraw the money in case of emergencies, or for gratification of other desires like purchasing a car. They also discontinue the SIP when market is in a bear phase. The long-term objective can be met only if we keep investing till the end of the term.

That's why I am proposing *SIPs IN REAL ESTATE.* SIPs in real estate means that you should make an investment in real estate and take it to its logical end by paying out EMIs right until the end. This is possible because as investors, you tend to stay invested in real estate for a longer period and you don't sell the property when real estate market is down. This translates into making a systematic investment, in real estate by way of EMIs.

"Real estate investing, even on a very small scale, remains a tried and true means of building an individual's cash flow and wealth."
– Robert Kiyosaki

UNDERSTAND THIS EXAMPLE OF
SIP IN REAL ESTATE:

1. Suppose you buy a commercial property worth INR 50 lakhs, by making a down payment of Rs 10 lakhs.

2. You take a loan of INR 40 lakhs for fifteen years period and at 10 percent your EMI amount would be INR 43,000.

3. If you rent out this property on a R/P ratio of 6 percent you will get INR 25,000 as monthly rent.

4. If you deduct this rent amount from your EMI amount, you will have to pay INR 18,000 as a difference amount toward paying EMIs.

5. We can call difference amount as your SIPs in real estate.

6. This amount will be decreased by 5 percent Y-O-Y basis every year, as you will get 5 percent escalation in rent every year.

7. Generally, in case of SIPs in mutual fund experts tell you to increase your SIPs by 5 percent every year.

8. If you sell the property in fifteen years, you will get INR 2.08 crores as large amount in hand.

ON THE OTHER HAND, THIS IS HOW SIP IN MUTUAL FUNDS WORK:

1. Suppose you make a lump sum investment worth INR 10 lakhs in a Balanced MF, and start a SIP of Rs 18, 000 for 15 years.

2. Value of your one time investment amount of INR 10 lakhs is INR 41.77 lakhs and value of investments in SIP is INR 72.29 lakhs

3. This amount will get you a corpus of INR 1.14 crores at the end of 15 years.

4. At the end of 15 years, your net gain will be INR 71.60 lakhs.

Studying the chart given below will enable you to understand the difference between the returns you will scoop up when you invest SIPs in real estate vis-à-vis your returns when you pursue long term SIPs in Mutual Funds. The results are stark.

WHICH IS THE BETTER
WEALTH BUILDER ?
**SIP IN REAL ESTATE
OR SIP IN MUTUAL FUNDS**

SIP in Real Estate	SIP in Mutual Funds
COST OF PROPERTY **Suppose you buy a 50 Lac property** **(office)** with a Down Payment Rs. 10 Lakh and take a 40 Lakh Loan at 10% for 15 years. The EMI is Rs. 43,000/-	**TOTAL INVESTMENT** **If you invest Rs. 10 Lac as lumpsum** **in a Balanced Fund** with a 10% return and also do a SIP of Rs. 18,000/- pm for 15 years
Down Payment (DP) **Rs. 10 Lakh**	**Lumpsum (One time investment)** **Rs. 10 Lakh**
Monthly SIP in Real Estate (EMI Rs. 43,000 - Rent Rs. 25,000 pm) **Rs. 18000/-** EMI - Rent = Net Outflow - **(SIP)**	**Monthly SIP in Balanced Fund** **Rs. 18000/-** Every month for 15 years
Loan Repaid (EMI Rs. 43,000 pm x 180 months) **77.40 Lakh**	**Value of investment** after 15 years is same as Corpus
Rent Received Rs. 25,000 pm with 5% escalation in Rent on Y-O-Y basis for 15 years **64.70 Lakh**	**Value of lumpsum (10 Lakh)** **41.77 Lakh** **Value of SIPs** **72.29 Lakh**
Total Value of Property after 15 years @ 10% appreciation in price **2.08 Cr.**	**Total Value of Corpus** after 15 years **1.14 Cr.**
Net Outflow (DP + EMI - Rent) **22.70 Lakh**	**Net Outflow** **42.40 Lakh** (Lumpsum + SIPs)
NET GAIN (Current Value - Net outflow) **1.85 Cr.**	**NET GAIN** **71.60 Lakh** (Total Value - Net outflow)

KEY TAKE AWAY :

By investing SIPs in Real Estate your wealth grows 9 to 10 times compared to the total
investment made, you also got 2.5 times more return compared to SIPs in Mutual Fund.

Case Studies

Throughout my book, I have laid emphasis on wealth creation using an innovative portfolio of properties. I am sharing a few live examples with you to highlight how smart real estate investment has benefitted investors.

Mr. Umashankar Modi- An entrepreneur who reaped rich dividends in land holding

In 1975, Mr. Umashankar Modi had purchased a 2.5 acre plot on the outskirts of Thane for INR 11.5 lacs. He has been consistently renting out this piece of open land over the last forty years and presently enjoys a monthly rent of INR 30 Lacs. The current value of the plot is over INR 100 crores. Mr. Modi also invested in an apartment in South Mumbai for INR 26 lacs in 1979, which is worth over INR 40 crores as per current market valuations.

Raju Gandhi- Making smart choices in picking up apartments

Mr. Gandhi's father had bought an apartment for INR 10,000 in Mulund in 1975. In 2001, opportunity presented itself once again when the adjacent apartment came up for sale. Mr. Gandhi moved in quickly to buy this apartment for INR 6.5 lacs in 2001. Today, both apartments are worth one crore each enabling Gandhi to make a windfall gain on the first apartment and also gain handsome profits on the second one.

Dipti Nimbalkar- A bold and risk taking woman who preferred property over gold

Dipti bought an office space for INR 8 lacs in 2005, selling all her gold worth INR 4 lacs against the wishes of her family. With the money from the gold, she arranged the down payment and took a bank loan for the rest of the amount. The loan was serviced from the rental income that the property started generating. The current value of the property is INR 80 lacs. Her husband who was working with a multinational company resigned and started his own company a few months back. He needed a workplace to operate the business and also capital amount to invest in it. Both his needs were met by the same property that Dipti had purchased in spite of the stiff resistance from her family. Not only did he get an office space to operate his business from but he also got a business loan by mortgaging the same property with the bank. Now he is applauding the unconventional yet timely decision taken by his wife.

The Author's Story- One of foresight and sensibility

A plot of 2000 square feet was bought by the author's mother for INR one lac in Solapur in 2001. This was quite a rare step for a simple woman who had zero exposure to real estate. The open plot is worth INR 35 lacs currently making her the owner of a tidy sum.

I have shared a few examples here, but we have numerous such examples that have never made headlines. They are nevertheless success stories scripted by common and not so common people.

But we do not want to stop here. We want to hear personal stories about real estate purchases made by you. So I request you to send me your stories on my email id, **author@amjadkhan.co.in**, so we can publish some of your stories in this section in the forthcoming edition.

Disclaimer

All information, techniques, and concepts introduced herein are of general comment. The intent is to collate diverse information so as to provide a wide range of choices to the reader today and in the future, recognizing that there can be diverse circumstances and viewpoints for the same.

Should the reader decide to make use of the information contained within this publication, it will be their sole discretion and the author, publisher, and contributors do not assume any responsibility under any circumstances or conditions.

All the figures written in the charts and tables are indicative and have been calculated as per the different regions and market conditions. The author is presenting a personal viewpoint and is not contesting the figures given out by any governmental institution or competent authority.

Some banks do not allow renting out property mortgaged to them, so take permission from your bank before renting out your place.

L.R.D: Every bank has their own policy toward Lease Rent Discounting Scheme, so please check with the bank's L.R.D rules before finalizing any property.

Bank Loan: Loan to buy any property is given at the sole discretion of the bank subject to your credentials like income, cibil score etc.

You would need proper permission license and tax registration to start an air bnb/hostel/studio apartment/serviced apartment/ tent house/marriage lawn etc. services in india.

If you enjoyed reading this book..

Check out my website
www.amjadkhan.co.in/book

I would also love to hear your feedback!

Write to me at
author@amjadkhan.co.in

About Success Gyan Publishing

We believe that everyone has knowledge to share and lessons to teach and what better way to do so than through a book.

Success Gyan Publishing, a publishing house formed with the mission to bring out the creative genius within everyone, aims to simplify the book publishing process for those who wish to share their knowledge through books.

Earlier, if you were to write and publish a book, you needed an agent to get a publishing house to look at your manuscript and even then there was no guarantee that they will publish your book.

Now, if you're wondering if there's a better way, there most certainly is. You can now take control of your book and how it is published through the Success Gyan Publishing platform. From planning your book cover to setting a timeline, the SGP team makes this daunting journey to becoming an author.

We are on a mission to help business owners and professionals to bring out the book in them, and help them transform their business or profession, by becoming an author.

Website - www.sgpublication.com
Email - info@successgyan.com